CREATIVE
SPACES

People,

Homes,

and

Studios

to Inspire

CREA
SP

TIVE ACES

Ted Vadakan & Angie Myung

with Gregory Han

Photography by Ye Rin Mok

CHRONICLE BOOKS
SAN FRANCISCO

Library of Congress Cataloging-in-Publication Data:

Names: Vadakan, Ted, author. | Myung, Angie, author.
Title: Creative spaces : people, homes, and studios to
    inspire / by Ted Vadakan and Angie Myung ; with
    Gregory Han.
Description: San Francisco, CA : Chronicle Books LLC, 2019.
Identifiers: LCCN 2018056046 | ISBN 9781452174099
    (hardcover : alk. paper)
Subjects: LCSH: Artisans—Homes and haunts. | Interior
    decoration—History—21st century—Themes, motives.
Classification: LCC NK2115.3.A76 V33 2019 |
    DDC 747.009/05—dc23 LC record available at
    https://lccn.loc.gov/2018056046

Manufactured in China.

Design by Vanessa Dina and Ly Tran.

10 9 8 7 6 5 4 3 2 1

Chronicle books and gifts are available at special quantity discounts to corporations, professional associations, literacy programs, and other organizations. For details and discount information, please contact our premiums department at corporatesales@chroniclebooks.com or at 1-800-759-0190.

Chronicle Books LLC
680 Second Street
San Francisco, CA 94107
www.chroniclebooks.com

Dedicated to our moms

FOREWORD BY JAIME DERRINGER OF DESIGN MILK

I GET ASKED ABOUT my office a lot. People want to see it, photograph it. As I'm someone who spends all day looking at (and often curating, judging) beautiful spaces, curiosity about my own space arises. But—sadly—I am the cobbler with holes in her shoes. My office, which is technically a spare bedroom in my home, has always been a plain box filled with whatever furniture survived the move from one house to the next. The truth is I've been too busy working, building Design Milk, nurturing it, and sacrificing my own needs for its benefit. That's probably why I like to peek into other people's spaces with such voyeuristic joy. As Design Milk has grown, I've slowly started working on my own home, making it a place that reflects who I am. Maybe one day I'll get around to designing my dream office . . .

Our spaces are supposed to reflect who we are. Whenever I am asked for decorating advice, I typically say, "Buy only things that you love." I want to encourage people to be creative and personal with their spaces, to surround themselves with objects that they love, that have meaning, that tell stories, not shop for everything at one store or buy things simply to fill a space or a blank wall. I want to walk into a home and immediately get a feel for who lives there, and not confuse it with a model home or a catalog set. We should all think of our home as our favorite pair of jeans—comfortable, relaxing, fits like a glove, but most of all it feels like HOME.

I've long been a fan of Poketo and how they're creating a beautiful, creative community in Los Angeles. I admire their dedication to good design and their desire to help others fill their homes with meaningful objects. But Angie and Ted take it to another level through their understanding that design comes from and is for humans. The workshops, programming, in-person events, and pop-ups shine a light on how design is so much more than objects, and that bringing people together to collaborate or to be more creative is just as critical to design and community as swinging a hammer or buying a rug.

When they asked me to write this foreword, I started thinking about *why* it is that we love seeing other peoples' spaces. I already told you that I love looking at them because I still have a lot of work to do myself—yes, part of it is pure inspiration. But I think there's more to it. I believe that what we choose to surround ourselves with is a reflection of our humanity. We want to see parts of ourselves in others so we can connect with them on any level . . . whether it's through a mutual love of Greek pottery, an admiration of Frank Lloyd Wright, or perhaps more importantly, the realization that we're not alone in not being able to get it all magazine ready and picture perfect.

What Poketo is doing by sharing these creatives' stories and spaces is giving us an exclusive peek behind the curtain. By doing so, we're reminded that there's a human being (or multiple humans) behind every little thing that we touch, every object or structure that surrounds us. Someone had an idea, and someone used their hands, brains, tools, and sweat, and maybe even some blood and tears, too, to birth this creative "something" into the world. Moreover, the spaces reflect how these people live their lives—a visual way of expressing their daily routine, how they relax, what supports their creativity, and, in some cases (like my own), how the creative struggle is *very* real.

With this book, Poketo is painting a full-spectrum picture of these creative individuals, so as you're reading this right now, you can hold a little part of their creativity, and humanity, in your hands.

INTRODUCTION

THIS IS NOT SIMPLY AN INTERIORS BOOK, but a celebration of creatives, their work, and their spaces, and an inquiry about their personal and professional philosophies. A creative space can be a home, a studio, or any inspiring environment. A creative's space is a living and breathing thing, evolving and reflective of its occupants. The definition of a creative is open to interpretation and debate, but this book focuses on artists, designers, cooks, writers, musicians, educators, architects, entrepreneurs, and others who strive to live artful, intentional lives, and explores the relationships these creatives have with their spaces.

Poketo's story can be told through various spaces. In 2012, while searching for a new and bigger workplace, we happened upon an empty storefront not far from our loft in the Arts District in Los Angeles. At 4,000 square feet, it was nearly four times larger than our loft, offering us a considerable amount of room to grow. But this was a big and frightening step for us. The rent was higher, the space was larger than what we needed, and the neighborhood was in a state of transition, still a bit of a ghost town offering very little foot traffic. What we did like was that this was a ground-floor unit; we would be able to put our sign on the street. We could open a Poketo retail store and the community space we had always dreamed of. So, despite our trepidation, we signed the lease, moving our entire operation into the new location.

We designed the office and retail store ourselves, erecting partial walls to separate the large space in two. We constructed custom retail fixtures on casters, allowing us the ability to reshape the store depending on the art show or event. We frequently hosted art events, talks, and creative workshops to engage and inspire our community, and now we had the room to organize the space according to the needs of the event rather than the other way around.

Our home life is very different, however. People assume our home is filled with beautiful furnishings and design objects—things you would easily find at Poketo. But when we leave Poketo for the day, we come to a home that's minimal, almost bare except for a very few items from our travels and friends. All the walls are white; there is no visible artwork displayed on the walls. We want a respite from looking at objects and thinking about design and colors all day long. We do have objects and furniture from designers we admire in our home, like the outdoor chairs by Sean Knibb and the beautiful ceramics by Tracy Wilkinson. Each of these things reminds us of our creative community, our friendships, and the value that creativity brings to our lives and spaces.

When we started Poketo in 2003, our first place was a tiny studio apartment in San Francisco across from Dolores Park. Poketo began as a side project shoehorned between the demands of work and school. We'd attend our friends' art shows, where countless examples of beautiful work would draw crowds at the opening but wouldn't sell. The observation inspired an idea: What if we could create something representing their work to carry everywhere around with you at a price anyone could afford? So we began making wallets with our friends' artwork. We ended up launching and selling out that first batch of wallets at an art show. Gradually, that first product turned into hundreds more, giving birth to our guiding principle of accessible, utilitarian, and beautiful designs for "art everyday."

After Angie finished art school, we decided to move from San Francisco to Los Angeles into Ted's parents' home for a year, where we focused all of our time and energy into growing this side project into a full-time job. Focusing solely on Poketo allowed us to source manufacturing in Los Angeles in order to add many new Poketo designs. A year later we bought our first home in Echo Park, news eliciting an unforgettably gleeful response from Ted's parents: "We get our house back, we get our house back!"

Our first home was modest, with a tiny kitchen, two small bedrooms, and a large master bedroom. Best of all, it had two large garages, perfect for storing all our goods. We ended up converting the master bedroom into the office, where we'd work many long days, but boxes of Poketo inventory multiplied, aggressively taking over our living room and office. Since we lived and worked in the same place, we lost any separation between home and work life. Artist friends—the types used to the craziest, most makeshift industrial live/work conditions—often would look around our house and ask us, "How do you live like this?" That's when it dawned on us that we needed to find another place for work.

In 2007, we moved our office into the top floor of an airy loft in the Arts District, the most eastern part of Downtown Los Angeles. We were now able to establish a real separation between work and home, affording us more opportunities for hosting events and the ability to hire a full-time staff of five to help us with our growing business. But as quickly as relief arrived, our once airy and immaculate loft again turned into a monster mess.

In 2012, recognizing we had outgrown our space yet again, we opened our first shop nearby in a burgeoning section of the Arts District, establishing Poketo not only as a brand, but also as a retail destination. Numerous awards and best-shops features in L.A. lists, as well as in *Wallpaper** and Monocle's travel guides, soon followed. By 2018, we had opened several stores across Los Angeles. Each of our spaces has evolved over the years. In hindsight, we can see how each Poketo space closely mirrors a moment in our lives.

This book explores the connection between individuals and space, whether that space is a home, studio, or both. In writing this book, we discovered everyone is in a state of "work in progress." A home, studio, or office of a creative is rarely static; it changes perpetually as needs, inspirations, and desires arise. We are all constantly in flux—a sign of growth, both personally and professionally.

Our spaces reflect our personal joys, hopes, dreams, evolution, work, inspirations, and aspirations in operating Poketo. There's a poster hanging in the home/studio of set designer Adi Goodrich and director Sean Pecknold that sums up everything we've learned over the years: "Everything yields to diligence." So true. Every person featured in this book epitomizes an ultimate work ethic; their persistence and perseverance are hallmarks of their success and happiness, and their inspiring homes and work spaces are reflective of the journey as well as the destination.

"We made an intentional decision to make our home the opposite of our work life."

SONOKO SAKAI

COOKING TEACHER AND AUTHOR

Highland Park, Los Angeles

BUCKWHEAT FLOUR, ALL-PURPOSE FLOUR, tapioca starch, water. By all standards, it's an unremarkable list of individual ingredients. But in the hands of Sonoko—educator, author, and consummate artisan soba noodle maker—the succinct recipe has never been an impediment to her imagination. "Every time I make noodles, they come out a little different. The ingredients are always the same, but there are numerous variables involved. Even the temperature of the hands can change the outcome," she says, glancing up for a beat before returning to the rhythm of kneading. When we first began hosting creative workshops at Poketo, we knew we wanted to expand upon the traditional definition of an artist to include a wider range of talents, but all sharing a dedication to creativity. In this way, Sonoko embodies an artist who just happens to work in an edible medium.

Angie first caught wind of Sonoko in 2008. Back then, Sonoko was just beginning to teach workshops at our neighborhood organic grocer, utilizing the skills she learned while studying soba-making in Japan. Sonoko had left a decades-long career as a film producer to become a writer and teacher, introducing soba noodles and the technique for making them to an entirely new audience in Los Angeles. We reached out to Sonoko years later with the proposal of hosting a soba-making class at Poketo. She agreed after attending one of our other workshops, appreciating the energy and community, and her own workshop sold out in a matter of days.

Standing shoulder to shoulder with attendees, we were mesmerized by Sonoko's confident and precise technique, following her guidance to transform our four ingredients into springy and complex noodles. Genuine buckwheat-flour soba noodles are earthy and texturally satisfying, and taste absolutely nothing like the packaged "soba" noodles found at the supermarket. "That's just flour with food coloring added," she says.

Sonoko is already sifting flour when we first enter her home, located in the Los Angeles neighborhood of Highland Park. She's readying a snack of plain soba accompanied by a dipping sauce of seasoned stock we will soon sit down to share. It is a simple meal, prepared with the measured efficiency of someone who could do this with her eyes closed. So it is somewhat ironic that the modest method unfolding before our eyes happens upon a grandiose stage—a table built by her husband, accomplished artist Katsuhisa Sakai. The table was tailored specifically to Sonoko's dimensions and movements, a platform of purpose and process for making and teaching. A shelf underneath offers a place for her to lodge her collection of bowls, knives, baskets, brushes, and rollers, a cast of tools that magically appears throughout the preparation we'll witness. The table's combination of form and function preludes the rest of the couple's life inside these walls.

"This table is large, but it can be moved easily for my work-shops. A lot of our furniture is made to be moved around as needed," she explains, noting that hosting classrooms and workshops regularly within your own home requires an adaptable interior, if not an adaptive personality.

The entire house breathes with thoughtful purpose. Their work requires organization, with tidy collections of bowls, cookware, and jars of fermented foods that will eventually make their way into Sonoko's cooking. What seems like a handmade lantern floating over the dining room table turns out to be a salvaged lampshade patched and turned upside down, an example of the couple's devotion to extending the life of any object invited into their home. Fermentation jars, books, and a few objects of sentimental history congregate in corners of the house. "I was able to make a place for some sentimental objects I've kept over the years by giving them newfound purpose," Sonoko says.

Inside this Southern California home, light and negative space operate as quiet partners with the couple's spare collection of furniture. The overall effect isn't austere, but one where it feels life is enjoyed without distraction. The few furniture pieces within their home seem to have arisen from the floor as naturally as geological formations. Warm sunlight enters the front of the home through their westward-facing windows, while the rooms in the back harbor a sanctuary of shade.

This is not to say the house is barren. Sonoko's insistence for preserving memory keeps the home rooted in the realm of the domestic rather than the monastic. In the kitchen a lone black-and-white photograph of her grandmother's Japanese kitchen adorns the wall, afforded a special place so Sonoko can always revisit the memory and be guided by it. "Look carefully and you can see I've arranged my kitchen to look as close to hers as I can. I have even placed my tools hanging the same way she did . . . I'm hoping to re-create the view out the window, too," she says, looking into their courtyard where several of Katsuhisa's statues stand sentry along a leaf-covered path leading to the backyard. "This house is a work in progress. There's still so much to do. I have dreams for a garden soon."

Miso Soup with Sonoko Sakai

Ingredients
One - 6-in Kombu Seaweed
1/3 brick of soft tofu, diced
2 cups of Bonito flakes
12 snow peas
3 1/2 tblsp miso paste, red n white
4 1/2 cups of water
1/2 cup scallions, chopped

↑
Bonito

1. Steep the Kombu in water over medium heat. Just before the water boils, pluck out the Kombu. (you can eat the Kombu n compost!)

2. Turn heat to Low, then add the Bonito Flakes. Let the Bonito flakes steep gently like tea for 2 minutes.

3. Strain the liquid in a sieve lined with cheese cloth. This amber colored liquid is your broth "Dashi".

4. Pour the Dashi in a sauce pan and bring it to a boil. Add the snow peas and diced tofu and lower heat to a simmer.

5. Thin the miso paste with a little Dashi. Add enough miso to the Dashi for good flavor. Some miso pastes are saltier than others so taste and make adjustments.

6. Divide the soup between four bowls and serve, garnished with scallions.

Enjoy! Sonoko

A NOURISHING START

We asked Sonoko to give us a favorite, everyday recipe. Miso soup is something she makes for herself every morning. What a nourishing and warm way to start each day. This recipe is simple enough for anyone and so delicious.

LILY
STOCKMAN

TEXTILE ARTISTS

Atwater Village, Los Angeles

HOPIE
STOCKMAN

BLOCK SHOP IS A DECEPTIVELY SMALL OPERATION, a brand producing some of the most beautiful woodblock-printed textiles today, with a team of just five working from a studio in the Los Angeles suburban enclave of Atwater Village. Their hand-printed products have become more popular and ubiquitous with every passing day, no doubt due to the fact they're consummate collaborators who've teamed up with a diverse cast of influential hoteliers, dressmakers, chocolatiers, and retailers, each drawn to Block Shop's inimitable organic, geometric motifs. It's really just two sisters—Lily and Hopie—there steering the ship. But they've diligently and strategically built a global company, one with its own dedicated team of artisans working in coordination with the sisters from a world away in Bagru, India.

It's easy working with Lily and Hopie. They represent our ideal, the type of small and socially minded business we most enjoy collaborating with. They're a company whose founders have made great efforts to integrate principles of community and sustainability into their business model that we strongly identify with at Poketo. The sisters adhere to paying wages 30 to 100 percent above local market piece rates and invest in numerous women's empowerment programs benefitting their workers; they're a company committed to investing in people more than anything else.

In forming friendships, there's a tendency to project our own hopes and values onto newfound friends. But in the case of Lily and Hopie, the simi-larities between us seem genuinely numerous. In these two we recognize

our own perpetual state of hustling—the entrepreneurial efforts required to realize whatever it is we're envisioning, to scratch that creative itch—while also, hopefully, positively impacting the world in the process. Sitting in their Los Angeles studio, surrounded by the splattered paint of past projects and neatly stacked piles of block-printed paper and fabric, the sisters tell us how they rely on a back-and-forth dialogue unique to their close kinship as sisters; they admit sometimes they're unable to recollect who was responsible for which decision, unbothered with being properly credited, an awesome example of the synchronicity and humility of their partnership. After all, the love between sisters doesn't always extend to a professional relationship, but these two have organically coordinated their individual skills into a concerted effort that sometimes makes them seem like a single entity. But they're not. Lily is an artist, a trained painter with a career distinct from Block Shop and her own separate studio; Hopie graduated with an MBA from Harvard Business School and empowered the business to become a community changemaker. Block Shop permits the sisters to collaborate on an equal footing creatively, approaching challenges from different but complementary perspectives.

The sisters founded Block Shop while still in grad school, a time when the pair plotted a business model before launching. They'd eventually borrow money from their mom to get things started, but also gave themselves a six-month goal to keep focused. Hopie would proudly share, "We've since paid it all back!"

So much of this book is dedicated to people who were formerly strangers, but who've became friends—sometimes slowly, sometimes quickly—through the transformative process of collaboration. The seeds of mutual admiration are usually already planted before any first exchange, especially here in Los Angeles, where word of mouth (and the algorithms of Instagram) can ignite connections with surprising immediacy. Block Shop is what happens when talent meets purpose, and working with them has given us a deeper appreciation of how to utilize strategized entrepreneurial efforts to enrich the lives of everyone working with and for us. Block Shop began as an art project more than eight years ago, one sparked by a move to India. Today, it's a thriving business, selling in more than sixty stores around the globe, providing jobs to three different families of master printers and two family-run weaving organizations in Jaipur and Panipat, and helping fund a plethora of social projects and services as beautiful as anything Block Shop designs. They've become our definition of the art and business of community.

Our collaborative history with Block Shop spans from product to workshop. Our Block Shop x Poketo exclusive textile scarf proved a rather challenging project, with the translation of our digital design into a handcrafted textile presenting unforeseen complications. But if there's anything true about Lily and Hopie, it's that they love a challenge. With the aid of their collaborative counterpart in Bagru—a master printer—the sisters were able to eventually turn a digital design into a beautiful handcrafted scarf we were proud to be associated with.

"Most of the time we try to have balance. I'm painting two or three days a week, in Block Shop two or three days a week. It's only getting harder, and I don't always know how to balance it all, but I love the insanity of it. Amid all the chaos, it's helpful to have these really clear deadlines and boundaries, then work it out."

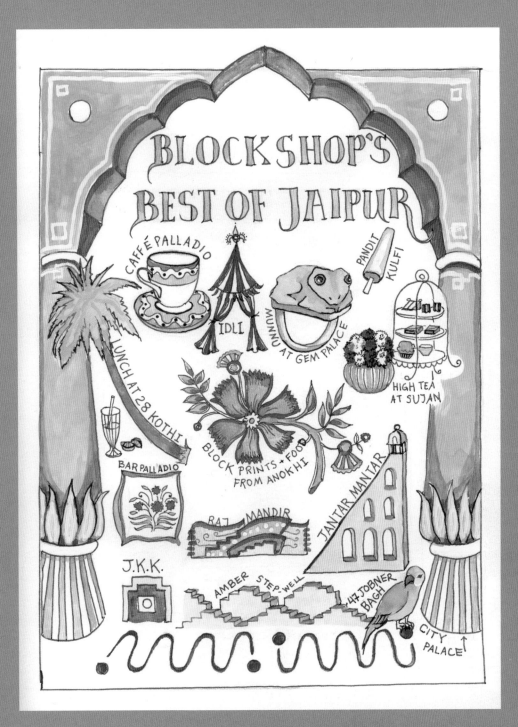

A SECOND HOME

Lily and Hopie travel to India often to visit their team in Jaipur and oversee production. We've always been enamored by their adventures, the sights and colors from their travels. We asked them to put together a map of their favorite, must-visit places. Not surprisingly, both sisters collaborated on the art for this map, as they do with everything in Block Shop.

DAVID IRVIN

CREATIVE DIRECTOR
West Adams, Los Angeles

"I don't mind dirt and rust, and I like things that don't look spanking new, because it adds a little bit more character."

SOME PEOPLE OPERATE with an unaffected air of casual cool that permeates everything they do. David is the epitome of this vibe—a creative director, graphic designer, artist, and surfer who can't and won't be pigeon-holed in any way, shape, or form. We first worked with David back in 2013 while embarking on the launch of our second Poketo store within the Line Hotel in Koreatown. With a reputation built upon working with numerous restaurant and hospitality projects, including Gjelina, Gjusta, and Hinoki & the Bird, David was tasked to design the Line's brand identity. We immediately recognized that his artistic and abstract approach to creativity, both personally and professionally, was inimitable.

The Line Hotel identity he eventually created was born from a simple hand-drawn line—a supremely unpretentious solution that emerged organically. It didn't feel like graphic design; it felt like art—which does a fair job of describing nearly everything David does. But the kicker is that David is one of the most down-to-earth human beings we know.

David lives in West Adams, one of the oldest and most unappreciated neighborhoods of Los Angeles, predominantly populated by an architectural parade of Craftsman, Victorian, Beaux Arts, Spanish Revival, and Queen Anne homes. Over the last few years West Adams has made a resurgence, witnessing the pros and cons of gentrification. David's address doesn't come as a surprise. In fact, it seems the perfect neighborhood for someone drawn to aesthetic eclecticism, cultural contrasts, and the patina of time.

Everyone invited to David's compound is greeted by an unusual architectural layout: a small house with a 1920s pedigree out front, a contemporary two-story main house in the back, and an additional one-story carport studio situated in between. David was able to purchase the two-house lot in part because he found it before the uptick in Los Angeles real estate prices, but mostly because nobody else was crazy enough to tackle the multitude of challenges the dilapidated property offered. David's plan from day one was to build his dream home to spec in the back while operating his creative agency, Folklor, from the smaller detached carport studio. He left the small house out front mostly intact, renovating the interior only to an extent he felt happy and comfortable with.

There's an easy comparison to be made here between home and owner—each comfortably wearing rough exteriors, changed by time, with friendly and calm interiors awaiting those fortunate enough to be invited inside. David and his fiancée, Lisa, live surrounded by their favorite books and a verdant collection of house plants. While the small house in the front retains the neighborhood's historical charm, the two-story house in back is undeniably modern, an industrial presence covered in a Corten steel facade that has taken on a burgundy patina. Apparently his neighbors didn't share his love for the corrosion of conformity, but David says he loves the observable transformation as the oxidation unfolds across the surface of his house year to year.

In keeping with this theme of embracing imperfection, David has left the interior wooden beams unfinished. The T-shaped supports hint at the space's past life as a parking garage and create a threshold between distinct spaces in what otherwise would be an open floor plan.

Careful inspection reveals different textures inside the airy open layout: teak, ipe, sealed concrete, and marble. "Look, there's like five, six, maybe even seven different types of wood inside here," David admits. "I just love different woods together." He seems content to do things for their pleasure rather than according to anyone else's definition of right or wrong. Thanks to this interplay of textures, the interior is subtly stimulating and deceptively simple, a credit to David's eye for finding the similarities among the differences.

The house reflects David's confidence in mixing and matching contemporary with midcentury and vintage furnishings. All together it's a breezy, modern West Coast home, an atmosphere mirrored across the city over at the Native Hotel in Malibu, a project David conceived and executed. The sunshine-kissed shoreline of Malibu may feel a world away from historical West Adams, but David's hotel glows with the same casual comforts and surfer vibes as his own home.

"I just feel like, at age forty-seven, I've finally become comfortable in my own skin. It's okay to be a little weird and let go. I now recognize I can make mistakes, but now I'm actually learning from the stumbles. If you don't try, what's the point?"

STEPHEN KENN

BEKS OPPERMAN

AS A MARRIED COUPLE running a business together, we have a real soft spot for Stephen and Beks. We see a lot of ourselves in their personal and working history, recognizing many of the same challenges and rewards the couple has experienced over the years living, loving, and working together. We met them back at one of the informal, word-of-mouth events they'd host, called the Backdoor Coffee Club and the Backdoor Cocktail Club, the sort of social gatherings remembered for their invigorating conversations, delicious cups of coffee, and precisely mixed cocktails.

Stephen and Beks operate in a dynamic partnership, a multidimensional relationship reflected in the place they call home—an industrial loft still wearing some of the fading details of its furniture factory past. Located in a fairly desolate and rough-hewn part of Downtown Los Angeles, and only a few minutes away from the couple's separate working studio, their loft houses a handsomely appointed and partitioned living space within. Its evolution over the years has been guided by a set of rules the couple established to help them steer away from easy options and toward lasting, meaningful solutions adaptable to their daily needs. "It's still very much in progress, and it sometimes feels like a really fun, long-term art project . . . something like playing with Legos," says Stephen. He goes on to point out how he designed the sectional sofa, chaise, and coffee table for optimal modularity and movement, their combination allowing somewhere in the ballpark of forty different configurations to suit their needs.

As the day fades into the later afternoon, a corner of their living room takes on the warm hue of waning sunlight entering through a curtain-framed window, illuminating their vintage and midcentury furnishings. Just to the side of the window, an in-wall bar cabinet contains more than a hundred

whiskies the couple has collected on their numerous adventures around the world (the two are also passionate motorcyclists who have rented bikes all over the globe).

As enamored as we are with their whiskey, it proves nearly impossible not to gravitate toward the defining feature of Stephen and Beks's interior: vast floor-to-ceiling shelving that covers half the length of one wall, displaying tableware and so many books that a sliding ladder is required to reach the highest copies of their collection. Stephen says they're mostly Beks's books and notes that even though they're regularly strapped for time, Beks, a voracious reader who habitually carries a book everywhere, still somehow finds a way to read sixty to eighty books per year. It's evident these two love collecting, but how they've managed to incorporate these objects into textural, colorful elements of décor is a credit to their eye for livable design.

Stephen originally moved from Canada to the United States to begin a new chapter as a furniture designer after years working in fashion. Today, Stephen Kenn Studio in Downtown Los Angeles manufactures timeless midcentury furnishings with a vintage military-issue aesthetic created using canvas and leather. The catalog doesn't imitate the past but respects the best of it as applicable solutions for how we might live today. But like many designers, Stephen's greatest strength has always proven to be in the creative, not in the minutiae of management or business development. That's where Beks's expertise has become a vital step. We can't help but make an analogy to furniture: Stephen as the cushions offering shape, Beks the supportive frame and stitching keeping it all together.

With a background in the medical profession (nothing gets more serious than working in the ICU!), Beks brings a sharpened talent for organization, operations, and getting shit done to the daily operation of the design studio. As a self-professed analytic, left-brained personality, Bek became involved in Stephen's business organically, complementing his right-brain inclinations and allowing him the freedom to focus on what he's best at.

Even if Beks and Stephen's working dynamic wasn't the consequence of a conscious or strategized plan, it has been essential for the company's growth. It was only after several years of heading operations that Beks came to realize her role and importance as a chief entrepreneur. "The thing is, this didn't begin as a dream of mine like it did for Stephen. I just kind of fell into it." It's an admirable example of two people helping lift each other forward toward a common goal as necessity requires.

Though their home is a cornucopia of interesting objects attached to an assortment of fascinating stories, it's an easily looked-over object both Stephen and Beks pick out as their favorite—a little stump made by Max Lamb for *My Grandfather's Tree*, a collection of pieces made from a tree from Lamb's grandfather's yard. "It's not that the log is valuable in any way. But through the process of documentation and story, it has a meaningful connection to the past. I love legacy in that respect—the humility and realness in our lineage."

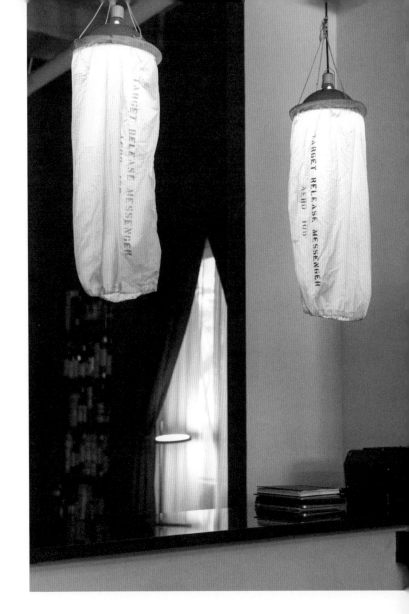

HELEN LEVI

CERAMICIST

Red Hook, Brooklyn

HELEN HAS A THING for unwanted plants. She loves taking in abandoned houseplants found along Brooklyn's curbsides or fishing them out of dumpsters—castoffs deemed hopeless and no longer worth the effort—and nursing each back to health in her apartment and studio. The hobby doesn't seem unusual for someone whose work as a ceramicist often offers plants a place to call home.

"Ya gotta keep trying . . . never give up," she tells us, pointing toward one of her more recent arrivals, already flowering happily with its second lease on life.

As a ceramicist, creative, and business owner—practically a one-woman army—Helen's words take the form of a matter-of-fact wisdom earned from someone who has had to pick herself up after tripping over a multitude of unforeseen hurdles. She's honest and humble enough to confess to a rocky start after graduating from Oberlin College, where she entered as a math major and emerged with a degree in photography, although she eventually found her current path as a well-regarded, in-demand ceramicist. The timeline she shares with us is painted with honest mistakes and hard-earned realizations we can completely empathize with, recognizing some of the same pitfalls we had to climb out of while establishing Poketo.

"I'm always trying stuff all of the time. I feel with ceramics the steps required to make them are really inspiring. Even with pieces I'll never make again, or mistakes, I like seeing how it all comes out."

"A year into my career, I ended up overdrawing from my bank account. I didn't recognize the operating costs of even my smallest efforts, and my parents had to lend me $3,000 to keep me afloat." Even though Helen kept her overhead low, working from a shared studio and using shared equipment, the costs related to making ceramics had drained her bank account empty. "Borrowing that money was a turning point. I literally needed to scrape bottom to arrive at this realization about operating a business."

Thankfully, it wasn't all pitfalls for Helen. She'd soon cross paths with an influential Manhattan boutique owner, who ended up placing what was to become Helen's first legitimate order. In turn, the opportunity motivated Helen to seek a separate studio. "Once I completed that order, I began believing I could really do this."

Shoehorned into a worn brick and timber commercial building out in Red Hook, Helen's studio resides in what she considers the last bastion of Brooklyn affordable enough for independent artists and designers to rent. The bare-bones building is peeling away from the inside out, made raw over the years from industrial use. Helen tells us the brick and concrete interior holds on to cold with a stubborn, chilly greed that then bakes hot during the summer months. But it's cheap, and the spacious 1,500-square-foot interior allows Helen to spin clay on her own wheels, fire up pieces from her own kiln, and stack inventory up to the ceiling. It's become a home away from home, splattered with paint and clay from the making of countless plates, bowls, mugs, and planters, with small curios and random objects lining shelves with the rhythm of musical notation. As dog owners, we take notice of the well-worn dog bed set to the side of her worktable, where her dog, Billy, waits out the long sessions that regularly unfold here.

If Helen's studio is spacious, the apartment Helen and her husband, Nick, call home is undeniably cozy. They live in a huge, old apartment complex in Brooklyn where the rent is reasonable, offering an increasingly rare opportunity for the young creatives to survive in New York. But it does come with trade-offs. "Neither of us has a desk. Nick will work from home sometimes, and he'll have to sit on the couch working. It would be nice to have a second bedroom for an office."

Inside, we notice Helen's proclivity to save what others may discard extends to her own creations. The apartment is populated with her own ceramic seconds—pieces with imperfections that keep them from being offered for sale. A collection of planters and mugs, many housing her adopted plants, dollop the apartment with cheerful color. The imperfections aren't as apparent as Helen's experimental attitude and love for process.

BEHIND THE LENS

Before Helen dove headfirst into ceramics, she was a photographer. Her incredible eye is apparent in both her photography and ceramics work. On the walls of her apartment, she has some of her favorite images blown up and framed, including these two. Even though she is a full-time ceramicist, she still identifies as a photographer. When you love something, you hold on to it.

"I took this photo at Great Sand Dunes National Park in southern Colorado. I was on a road trip at the time, visiting different ceramic factories that made some of the materials I use in the studio. It was about four years ago, when my business was starting to feel real for the first time. I know it's just a pretty landscape, but it represents a special time to me, transitioning from a photographer into this new career of mine."

"This photo was from the same road trip, nearby in Taos, New Mexico. I have loved road trips for a long time; my family used to take them when I was a kid, and when I was studying photography in college, having my grandmother's car was crucial for my photo projects, tooling around rural Ohio and discovering that kind of brand-new young-adult freedom. I pulled over on the side of the road to set up my medium-format camera and take this photo."

ADI GOODRICH

SET DESIGNER AND DIRECTOR
Atwater Village, Los Angeles

SEAN PECKNOLD

ONE OF OUR MOST MEMORABLE workshops was led by Adi, a Los Angeles set designer and art director whose portfolio is filled with larger-than-life sets, each imbued with surprise and wonder. She builds these sets primarily for advertising campaigns but also occasionally for music videos, most notably in collaboration with her fiancé, Sean, a filmmaker and animator (who also happens to be the brother of Robin Pecknold of the indie folk band Fleet Foxes). They seem a match made in heaven, dedicated to turning dreams into physical experiences through the studio they founded together, Sing-Sing.

Adi and Sean's Spanish bungalow sits on a rather quiet street of Atwater Village, a Los Angeles suburb known for its diverse cast of residential architecture and its proximity to the freeway, where cars flow barely faster than the adjacent Los Angeles River. The exterior of their duplex gives no indication of the large amount of space within and also out back (at least by Los Angeles standards).

"Art will always find a place in the world to live; you just have to make it first."

Welcomed inside, we ask about details like the hand-drawn quote tacked above Adi's bulletin board, "Everything yields to diligence," a reflection of her Midwestern appreciation for patience in cooperation with hard work. "We both believe that working hard is the best thing you can do. I mean, what else is there?" Whatever seriousness implied at the moment is humorously defused by another nearby drawing of a dismembered hand embellished with the cursive missive: "Let go."

"It's really important to have friends' work on our walls; it means we can look up and see them often, think about them in the world also making things and living the true hustle."

The couple's tastes and inspirations tend to overlap, occasionally diverging only to meet again. They cite the likes of Yuri Norstein, Mary Blair, Ettore Sottsass, Paul Klee, Henri Matisse, Jim Henson, Andrei Tarkovsky, Akira Kurosawa, Josef and Anni Albers, and Ellsworth Kelly as inspirations. Upon listing these favorites, Adi stops to reflect, "We love imagining artists of the past are our relatives or ancestors. These people paved the way, showing us what it means to be a working artist."

An improvisational rhythm rules here, characterized by the couple's preference for relaxed visual compositions. Colors and shapes spread out, abruptly stopping, to be continued again elsewhere. The décor is loosely strung together in literal and figurative fashion. A clutch of flowers held by the tapered neck of a colorful ceramic vase by Adi sits underneath a hanging garland of graphic cutouts. One piece particularly catches our attention, a "motion painting" originally made for the video for the Fleet Foxes song "Third of May / Ōdaigahara." It's one of seven different paintings made for the video, created using paint manipulated into movement with compressed air. "We think it looks like the shape and color of dreams, a fitting piece for above the bed," says Adi.

"For several years, we've been of the mindset that you always have to be moving. Everything in your body is moving all the time, and good things come when you're also moving. Creative breakthroughs often happen while you're walking; philosophical insights bubble up while traveling on a train," explains Sean. "The body wants to be in motion."

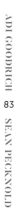

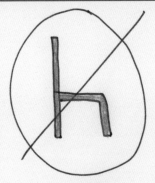

for too long
Sitting ˅ equals death

Eat mostly plants

Movement matters
most

Be in nature
with friends

Read for many hours
after coffee

Be your art
ancestors

MOVEMENT MATTERS MOST

We asked Adi and Sean what keeps them moving, what keeps them inspired. Sean immediately replied, "I think about how big the universe is and how fast it is moving outwards, expanding away from us faster than we could ever catch up with." Sean then quickly sketched on paper some of their life mantras. After glancing at them, Adi chimed in, "This is everything!"

BRENDAN RAVENHILL

DESIGNER

Echo Park and Glassell Park, Los Angeles

MEETING BRENDAN FOR THE FIRST TIME had all the trappings of a
first date. As is often the case, we were introduced to one another over
email by a mutual friend. We'd eventually meet at a local dive bar in Echo
Park, and over a few beers we discovered we had quite a lot in common
as creatives, business owners, and Angelenos. We're all as obsessed with
business as we are with design. Brendan may be first and foremost a
designer, known nationally for his signature lines of lighting, but he's also a
passionate business owner. In both endeavors he's distilled his process into
a three-word equation: input for output.

When we first met, Brendan was still working out of his Echo Park
home—a 1938 residence designed by acclaimed midcentury architect
Rudolph Schindler and built for just $6,000 at the time (even adjusted
for inflation today, that's still a reasonable $103,000 home). Brendan
now shares this home with his wife, Marjory, and their two-year-old son,
Ash. Brendan's current bedroom once operated as his work studio, with
the downstairs basement used as a toolshed. When he began, it was
mostly just him designing and constructing each piece to order, only
occasionally with the help of one part-time assistant. Today he operates
an impressive 14,000-square-foot warehouse with its own production
center, showroom, and office in Glassell Park. The lone vestige of his
former live/work lifestyle resides in the backyard toolshed, a space he's
set aside for hand-assembling frames for paintings and pictures—an
activity he describes as "tooling around."

Brendan's house was originally conceived as an affordable housing solution constructed with plywood, a material cheap even at that time. Despite its architectural pedigree, one attached to the Schindler name, the house fell under the radar of architecture historians and buffs. The relative anonymity allowed Brendan to slowly renovate and restore the home unbothered and guided—but not strictly—by Schindler's original design language. He ripped out the kitchen floors, along with the worn blue and pink plywood floors in the living room, replacing them with a beautiful linoleum in a shade that falls within Schindler's oeuvre, covering the room with a material ideal for the couple's child to play upon. Brendan admits he originally felt the pangs of buyer's remorse during this period, disappointed with the home's original institutional appearance. With its sharp interior angularity, it's not an easy interior space to furnish guided by contemporary standards or expectations. But once Brendan began furnishing the rooms with his own work, representing a modern, utilitarian, industrial aesthetic, he recognized his pieces had found a perfect harmonious setting within the academic beauty of Schindler's architecture.

Until the age of eight, Brendan lived in Côte D'Ivoire, where his father worked at the University of Abidjan, helping establish the West African Museum Project (WAMP) before becoming Chief Curator for the Smithsonian Institution's National Museum of African Art. Brendan was able to retain a single storage unit of art from his father's assembled collection, and much of it now furnishes his home today. He cites his father's original pieces as the most prized objects in his home.

If his home is still quietly waiting to reach its full potential, it could be argued the Brendan Ravenhill Studio in Glassell Park has exceeded it. The entire space follows the designing and manufacturing process: Areas defined for design, preproduction, production, and fulfillment run parallel to areas dedicated to administrative, marketing, and showroom purposes, meeting together at a communal, open kitchen that Brendan built out himself. It's an interior layout designed to allow people and product to continuously come together.

Not only has Brendan been able to continue pursuing his passion for designing, he's admirably been able to manage an ever-larger team, establish an inspiring work culture, and expand his brand and business to new markets. A couple of days a week, Brendan's team takes turns making communal meals for each other. When asked what they were making today, two of his employees said, "Watermelon salad and pasta. We don't have a stove top and we have to make lunch under forty minutes. But we always make it work."

"Input for output."

CHRIS MANAK

PRODUCER AND DJ
Montecito Heights, Los Angeles

IT SEEMS APPROPRIATE that music was the binding agent that brought Chris and us together. You have to rewind back to the late '90s, a few years before we began Poketo, to pinpoint the moment when our lives first converged. We were living in San Francisco; Ted was working at a music distribution company, his first job, one he will *always* remember as the worst place he's ever worked. Beyond youthful optimism and energy, the one thing that kept Ted returning to work day in and day out was the talented people he worked beside. It was here Ted would meet Chris, the founder of Stones Throw Records, a new hip-hop record label that would go on to help establish the West Coast hip-hop scene, domestically and internationally, releasing a legendary catalog of records from the likes of Madlib, J Dilla, and Madvillain.

Chris and his fiancée, Erika, now live only a few miles from us as the crow flies, in a hilltop home graced with the sort of magnificent view of Los Angeles that makes one unconsciously utter "wow" at first glance. It's a home filled with many distinguishable parallels to the uncategoriz-able music Chris performs as Peanut Butter Wolf: midcentury furnishings accented by thrift store kitsch, all anchored by the decorative rhythm of Erika's art. There are quirky details, too: Mayan-inspired doorway carvings and scallop-shaped walls, each remnants of its previous owners' eccentric visions. Instead of removing and renovating these vestiges of another time, Chris and Erika decided to embrace these details with their own posses-sions, a decorative remix across decades.

The home seems to have a palpable effect upon Chris. He's normally a shy and quiet person, but in the privacy of his own home with Erika and their beloved dog nearby, he's much more relaxed, verbose, and playful. Erika is a family therapist who uses art for healing, and she's quietly the heart and soul of the home they've built together in these hills of Northeast Los Angeles. Her paintings play prominently upon their walls, and their kitchen table also operates as her studio, its length covered with numerous pieces at various stages of completion. Even when she's absent, Erika's presence is always felt within each room, as if at any moment she'll come back to continue painting while Chris sits nearby sipping whiskey.

The couple is still settling into their home, and hope to create an addi-tional space where friends and family can stay for longer visits. The garden, also inherited from its previous owners, hosts a parade of local wildlife. A coyote comes regularly to lounge comfortably in their yard; birds hide in a thicket of succulents and cacti. Across the way a detached garage studio houses thousands of obscure records collected over the decades, "friends" etched with their own stories and memories, each waiting to be retraced by a record needle. All together the house feels like its own commune, a compound of modest spaces.

Over the years we've continued to collaborate with Chris creatively. We love how relationships like this can come full circle. But we'd be lying if we claimed we knew that chance encounter in San Francisco more than twenty years ago would lead to such a long-lasting and collaborative friendship.

When we asked Chris if there was a song that might represent the home he shared with Erika, he paused and replied, "I'll have to think about that." Hours later, while we were in his studio shooting portraits for this book and reminiscing about the time he met the daughter of Sly, of Sly and the Family Stone fame, Chris remembered the 1973 single, "If You Want Me to Stay."

"I think we might have found the soundtrack of your home," Ted said.

"Yes," he replied with an approving nod. "One of them for sure."

Forever Us - Crystal

Nont For Sale - Sudan Archives

Coming Home Again - Cracky

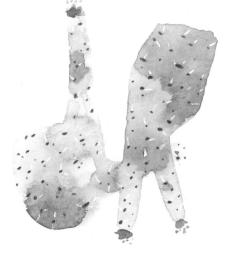

Rooms - Bryant K

Lady Love - Barrabas

BREAK IT DOWN

When we visited Chris and Erika's home, we were expecting nothing less than a library of music. Chris has described his vast record collection as weighing a ton. It's safe to say it's probably several tons. With music being at the forefront of their lives, we asked them to pick a few tracks that are the soundtrack to their home. They have eclectic and different tastes from one another. It took them some time to come up with a list of songs they both agreed on. The soundtrack they chose is a diverse mix of styles, not unlike their home and themselves. We love that Erika added a layer of art to each track, illustrating each one; a true collaboration between the two of them, turning music into visuals.

TAKASHI YANAI

ARCHITECT

Mar Vista, Los Angeles

WHEN WE ASKED TAKASHI to be part of this book, he told us he wasn't quite sure whether the one-story, postwar 1950s bungalow he called home was ready to be photographed; he was in the thick of renovating both the interior and exterior of the house, and there were still several ongoing projects yet to be completed. He kept us at arm's length with promises of "soon," but we were patient and persistent. Takashi eventually relented, and when the front door opened, all of our suspicions were proven, every expectation exceeded, our patience rewarded.

As a partner at Ehrlich Yanai Rhee Chaney Architects in Los Angeles, Takashi helms the firm's residential studio, designing multimillion-dollar dream homes built mostly unbridled from concerns about money, time, or resources. The same cannot be said about the home he's begun remodeling and shares with his wife, Patti, and kids, Emi and Kai. Constrained by a more modest budget (architects, they're just like us!), Takashi found himself at a crossroads: Sell the house and design something from scratch, or remodel their home of eight years and make it entirely their own.

Although there are elements of Takashi's professional strokes painted throughout the home—the fastidious level of attention to materials, the intentional use of light and shadow, an incorporation of indoor/outdoor living—the 1,500 square feet, originally built during the Southern California aerospace boom of the 1950s, invited loose, experimental solutions not always desired professionally.

"I spent the first half of my life being invited into other people's homes. Now I feel like I'm building a home to invite others into my life."

"My house is not like the work you see for my clients. I did everything opposite of what I usually tell them because I don't have the same budget," Takashi explained with a chuckle.

Those versed in the vernacular of traditional Japanese architecture might recognize elements of Takashi's heritage here and there, subtle references to childhood memories of Japan: The dark painted exterior may seem fashionably contemporary—and it is—but it also references an age-old process where timber is torched to a dark char, creating a protective carbonized finish called *shou sugi ban*. A backyard deck is as American as it comes, but here it is just long enough to accommodate sitting along its edge, operating as a floor-level bench and also as a transitional threshold between indoors and outdoors. And perhaps most conspicuous is the entire back wall, designed to open to expose the main living spaces to a continuous landscape view of the backyard garden, a hallmark of Japanese Buddhist temple architecture accomplished with frequent collaborator David Godshall, of the Los Angeles landscape architecture firm Terremoto.

"I've tried to make an effort to knock down walls in life to meet new people. I think I knocked down a real entire wall to let people in."

These details—including the initially controversial decision to paint the house all black on a street accustomed to varying shades of white or beige—have not gone unnoticed. But with time the tides have changed for the better. Takashi recollects how one morning, while he was enjoying his coffee, he overheard people speaking Japanese on the other side of his low front fence. He discovered an eighty-year-old Japanese woman had brought two of her fellow octogenarian friends to admire his home. They told him the house reminded them of the homes they'd grown up in back in Japan and were delighted to recognize their past in this home's present.

What we love the most about Takashi and Patti's home is its honesty. It's been remodeled with humble materials like plywood and metal, edited with little in the way of extraneous structural adornment that would take attention away from the view. The bookshelves running the length of the home from the front door to the back display a mesmerizing collection of books, toys, art, games, and various miscellaneous items belonging to the family, many tempting further inquiry. Ask Takashi about an object, book, or art piece, and he readily reveals a fond memory, interesting story, or impression of a friendship he cherishes. The only objects hidden from view are a meticulously arranged drawer of modernist kitchen utensils and a private collection of precious photography books stored away for safekeeping. But even these are readily shared if any inkling of interest is expressed. In this way, Takashi's home operates as an extension of his willingness to share much of his life, experiences, and expertise with open arms.

When we first met Takashi back in 2013, we had only recently opened our first Poketo store in the Los Angeles Arts District. Takashi was drawn by the buzz of potential clients and projects in the developing neighborhood, and he invited us to lunch to learn more about what was unfolding near and around us. We still remember he gave us a copy of a book, its pages filled with projects he and his firm had designed—relaxed and modern homes representing an aspirational level of beauty that wowed us immediately. It seems almost impossible years later to be working on a book together, showcasing his own home this time, its architecture no less aspirational and beautiful than anything we saw within the pages of his gift.

BLURRING THE LINES

Takashi's home is deeply influenced by Japanese culture. He worked in Japan before attending Harvard Graduate School of Design. Now, with global architectural projects, he finds himself traveling back and forth between home and new lands. Takashi is an accomplished photographer with a unique point of view. On a recent visit to Japan, we asked him to capture images that inspired him (shown here).

"I'm always inspired by the work that blurs the lines between architecture, art, and nature. Contemplative spaces like these put things in perspective and help us find our place in the world. I always return home energized and inspired to infuse future work with elements of the things I experience in my travels."

TAMMER HIJAZI

DESIGNERS
Brooklyn, New York

CAITLIN MOCIUN

SOME FRIENDS YOU MAKE by chance circumstance, while others arrive by the grace of an introduction by a good friend. If birds of a feather flock together, having someone seed the ground for the purpose of inviting a new friend is always welcome in our book. This happened to be the case when our bud (and talented designer) Eric Trine introduced us to Tammer while he was visiting from New York a few years ago. We had no idea at the time that the initial introduction would form a friendship with an incomparably talented couple sharing Poketo's love for the modern and graphic.

Tammer cofounded the Brooklyn design studio Bower with Danny Giannella back in 2013. We're fans of their experimental sculptural arrangements of elementary shapes turned into décor and furnishings. Many of their pieces have the appearance of being extruded from a two-dimensional plane—graphic silhouettes intended for serving, seating, or storage—optical illusions and planes of scale evoking Sol LeWitt, early 3-D animation, and maybe even the '80s video game *Q*bert*. Shortly after our initial introduction, we knew we wanted to work with them on some sort of collaborative effort; our love for their work seemed a motivation for working with Tammer and Bower Studios, resulting in an exclusive product for Poketo.

How amazing it was to discover his wife, Caitlin, also happened to be the founder, designer, and proprietor of Mociun, an acclaimed jewelry line and store we've long admired. Describing Caitlin's gift for combining stones and metals into a signature style representing the aesthetic and rational philosophies of the Bauhaus school is an academic oversimplification of the jewelry's beauty.

If the literary genre of magical realism represents an exploration of the real and imaginary, Tammer and Caitlin's shared home and their respective studios could all be described as examples of magical minimalism—spaces pared down to their essentials, yet also inhabited by phenomenal collections of objects reflecting their occupants' love for art, plants, and, of course, color. Occasionally the rooms are intersected by a measured moment of trompe l'oeil, mirrors that confuse and confound where spaces start and end. Some couples struggle to merge their distinct styles and preferences, producing a tangle rather than a weave, but this pair seems to have figured it all out, imbuing their rooms with the identifiable indicators of their distinct styles with harmonious equality. Later, when we visit each of their workspaces—Tammer's Bower Studios and Caitlin's Mociun retail shop and studio—we spot many of the same colors, patterns, materials, and textures that inhabit their domestic space. The aesthetic continuity of their home into their workspaces is an inspiring example of making work an extension, not a division, of a life.

While an all-white room offers the premise of clean modernity, too often a monochromatic space results in an impersonal effect. Simplicity is harder to pull off than it looks. Fortunately, in the hands of Tammer and Caitlin, their all-white walls operate as an agent of accentuation, an effective backdrop for all the playful color permeating their home: a pumpkin-hued couch, an orderly harlequin collection of ceramics mirroring the random patches of their terrazzo counters below, a library of book spines peeking out for inspection everywhere, a mullet of fabric wall art, and numerous objects collected from their adventures and from their counterparts within the Brooklyn design community. Numerous small curios perch here and there in colorful compositions that give ample space for each individual element to be appreciated (a consideration that hearkens back to Caitlin's expertise in retail and the minute details required in assembling jewelry). It's the sort of simple style that's actually very sophisticated and challenging to pull off, but Tammer and Caitlin do it with exceptional ease both at home and within their work spaces.

Our favorite moments within their home are the comforting and casual corners they've created for themselves. Obviously they've created a beautifully arranged home, but it's more impressive because it's been arranged for their lifestyle, not simply as a canvas for display. Of special note is a small corner of respite in which a pair of floor pillows and an altar of plants and a meditation bowl are overlooked by a multicolored wall hanging and a large arched mirror. The sum of these objects produces the embodiment of quiet self-reflection, offering the couple all the tools to welcome back calm into their minds when needed. It's admirable that in designing a space for it in their home, serenity is not something they merely wish for, but actively invite into their lives.

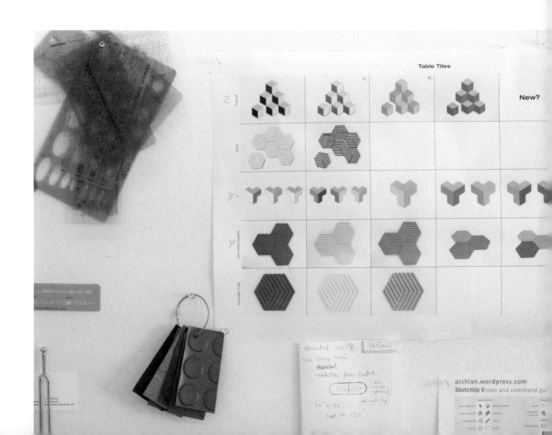

WINDY CHIEN

ARTIST
Mission District, San Francisco

AQUARIUS RECORDS on Valencia Street in the Mission District represents the quintessential San Francisco shop—the sort of independent retailer that leaves an indelible mark on your memories as a struggling twenty-something. While living in San Francisco, we'd flock to the record shop's bright and high-ceilinged interior to thumb through indie and electronic albums for countless hours. Aquarius was one of those small shops you'd call your home away from home. It was only years later, after we moved from San Francisco, that we'd discover Aquarius Records was owned by Windy—in hindsight, the connection between shop and owner suddenly seemed obvious.

The trajectory of Windy's life isn't a straight line but, instead, is as intricately woven as one of the textiles she's become renowned for: She was an army brat infected with a love of punk music while traveling across the nation, a passion that would lead her to become the owner of Aquarius Records for fourteen years. Her encyclopedic knowledge and expertise in music would eventually catch the attention of Apple, where she'd help build the fledgling iTunes and later their App Store into the media behemoths they are today. To describe Windy as a polymath seems an understatement. She's an omnivorous personality and someone whose life always seems to have yet another chapter to reveal.

An introductory macramé class provided the inspiration for something Windy would soon gain fame for—*The Year of Knots*—a knot completed every day, each documented on Instagram. She'd elevate the pragmatic purpose of a knot into a sculptural examination, but Windy says it was the satisfaction of tying a clean, tight knot that made the 365 days most fulfilling.

"You just have to keep doing the things that seem interesting to you at that moment in time. Then years later you'll be able to look back and say, 'Oh, now it all makes sense. All the dots connect!'"

Windy's house is impossible to miss, an Edwardian glowing bright with a progression of orange to red ombré paint visible from blocks away (another gradient of yellow to turquoise covers the backside). While the exterior is graphic and bright, the interior is decorated with the calm, organic palette of a passionate collector—a studied accumulation unaffected by clutter. We can travel only a few steps before stopping again and again to inspect Windy's collection of art, photographs, music, books, and musical instruments.

The living room is bathed in warm California light from the street-facing front windows, an element that adds to the cozy atmosphere she's made with her boyfriend, Gary. Windy leads us to the kitchen, where again her impeccable ability to organize and exhibit objects is on full display. A black spiral staircase leads up to the biggest surprise, a large master bedroom in the attic that runs the entire length of the house. When they moved in, the attic was an unfinished space, "just raw wood," Windy tells us.

Vaulted ceilings are challenging to work with. "You can't hang pictures off of a pitched roof ceiling," says Windy.

"Initially, I didn't know what to do, but then one day while I was staring up at the ceiling, inspiration came and I said, 'Gary, I've got it! Let's paint Pendleton stripes on the wall!'" Pendleton blankets draped across the bed further accentuate the length of the top floor rather than bring attention to its compromised height. Daring and brilliant.

When we finally make our way to the back of the house, we're given a view of the backyard, an overgrown patch allowed to grow free and wild. Having explored the entirety of the house, we realize Windy has arranged her home in parallel with her life, every bit as rich with texture and unrestrained energy as what she's shared with us this afternoon, room by room.

To be invited into Windy's Mission District ground-floor studio, just a ten-minute walk from her house, is to become immediately aware of how deeply she's immersed herself in her work. Every corner of the 800-square-foot space seems occupied with material dedicated to the exploration of the form and function of braiding fabric. Our eyes are drawn to the arrangement pinned to the wall, documenting the 365 days Windy dedicated to knots. Stacks of bucket-size spools of rope line floor-to-ceiling shelves, and woven baskets piled with thick braids of yarn sit like hand-pulled noodles awaiting Windy's creative appetite. Giant braided cords, punctuated at each end with a globe bulb, crisscross the ceiling overhead.

Windy's greyhound, Shelley Duvall, eyes us casually as we sit down in the middle of the studio's shag-covered floor to discuss Windy's work. Shelley Duvall's chill demeanor draws our attention, and Windy observes, "Greyhounds are like stoners. Super spaced out, super mellow. She's silent all of the time. She's a good studio dog. Aren't you?"

During our chat we breach a somewhat personal topic, but one we couldn't help but ask: "How does an artist make a living making knots in one of the world's most expensive cities to live in?" Practically speaking, she planned ahead by saving a year's worth of rent from her corporate job at Apple to pursue this artistic work. Giving herself a year to experiment proved a liberating strategy that has allowed her to envision an even bigger picture: larger arrangements, grander art installations, large-scale environmental pieces. She shows us CAD drawings intended for potential clients and institutions. Her *Year of Knots* has paid off.

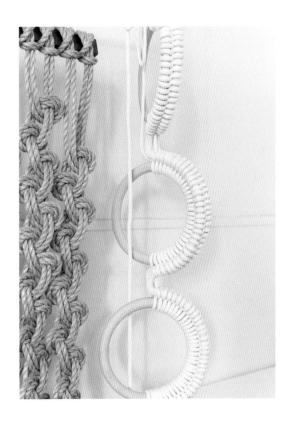

SHEV RUSH

KEVIN LANE

ENTREPRENEURS
The Sea Ranch, California

"The house kind of
tells us how to live."

IT'S NO HYPERBOLE to describe Shev and Kevin's Sea Ranch getaway as an awe-inducing architectural experience. A multitude of words and descriptions will drift onto and off the tip of the tongue throughout our tour of their home, situated among the trees of Northern California's most storied architectural community, but all will feel inadequate in capturing the unique space. Most people are fortunate to make a home for themselves. Our friends have carefully crafted an experience unique to this place, an archetypal architectural expression of everything we love about The Sea Ranch.

The particular charms of The Sea Ranch aren't unknown to us. It's where we escape to throughout the year when we want to clear our heads and refresh our bodies from city life. We're Shev and Kevin's neighbors for parts of the year in this intimate coastal community renowned for its distinctive coastal-modern architecture and evocative surrounding landscape, both of which are protected by strict edicts. An address here, perfumed by the saline splash of the Pacific and the silent embrace of trees, is less about ownership and more about a mutual agreement between place and person. Shev and Kevin are model adherents of this ideology (and owners of Placewares, a design shop and gallery in The Sea Ranch). The couple inhabits the Hines House—a 1969 William Turnbull Jr.–designed home and winner of the Sunset/AIA Home of the Year Award 1970—as occupants and stewards of the home, land, and history. Our friendship formed from a mutual love of design, nature, and adventure. They'd end up writing several local suggestions for us to explore before we left—listing secret beaches, hidden trails, and others spots formerly unbeknownst to us as first-time visitors. Of course, every one of their recommendations proved exceptional.

Shev and Kev would end up inviting us over to celebrate New Year's, introducing us to their home with a studied reverence of its history and an affection for all its unique details. They told us about the house's former owner—a peculiar and particularly detailed naval man with an affinity for nautical clocks and ship-worthy detailing they've kept in his honor. The kitchen and office/library were additions made according to Turnbull's design, with numerous pieces of décor left by the former owner continuing to find a home here. Even without the explanations and history, everything in this home exudes a permanence.

"It's not a house that you can sort of have junk thrown all over and live in casually or carelessly. It's a sort of a formal house, so we've decided to live guided by the architecture," notes Kevin, when we ask them about how living here differs from anywhere else.

The acquiescence is guided by a preservationist's heart and an appreciation of timeless design intended for use across lifetimes. But they're intrepid

renovators and dedicated to restoration, the type of architectural devotees willing to roll up their sleeves, pick up a hammer, and get their own hands dirty to repair and restore with exacting detail—believers in learning by doing.

At one point during our tour, they note that some visitors are prone to remark, "I'd put a big picture window there right in the middle of the beautiful living room wall to see the ocean." But for those patient enough to observe, the architecture reveals its thoughtful purpose. Long wooden planks extend floor to ceiling in the living room—each cut from a single slice of old-growth Douglas fir—a feature now too costly to reproduce today. Turnbull's vision extended upward to different levels and outward from entry into living room, presenting a view as immersive as the forest surrounding the home. Standing in the living room, where the ceiling reaches up to a neck-arching 27-foot height, the effect is intimate, like being in a forest. Another example: Some of the windows seem oddly placed, only to reveal their function over the span of the day, as sunlight casts a magical glow inside at certain hours. It's a fleeting moment, but intentionally so, a daily salutation to transient beauty. We're reminded of our own home and a stairwell window within. At a specific time, when the moon is full, but only at a certain time of the year, the luminescence of night spills into our home. Whether intentional or accidental, it's a reminder of how every home offers the opportunity for special moments, however fleeting.

SEAN KNIBB

ENVIRONMENTAL DESIGNER

Venice, Los Angeles

WE'LL ALWAYS REMEMBER the launch of a new hotel concept in Korea-town, now known as the Line Hotel, as a major turning point in Poketo's history. It was the year we signed on to what would become a colossal project in both scope and execution—a new hotel built upon the bones of midcentury architecture originally designed by Daniel, Mann, Johnson & Mendenhall. We were asked to help tear down LA's past to build its future. Of course we wanted to be part of this ambitious project! We'd be given a stake in the Koreatown hotel with our own outpost in the hotel's lobby—a smaller, distilled version of the Poketo retail and design experience for guests and locals alike. It was under these circumstances we met Sean of Knibb Design, the creative team brought in to reimagine the hotel experience of Los Angeles.

If you ask us what our impression of Sean was during our first meeting at his design studio in Venice, we might be inclined to pull out the "mad scientist" card. Some brains work with ideas from a singular and stationary focal point. Not Sean's. He seems perpetually brimming with crazy ideas, which he attacks from every angle, and is gifted at convincing collabora-tors to support them. From all initial observations, most of his ideas should not work, but somehow they not only succeed but also impart his designs with a layer of originality. He's never one to shy away from experimenta-tion, gifted with an ability to envision and harmonize contrasting colors, styles, and textures as energetic focal points within any space.

Several years ago, we were mulling over the idea of opening another Poketo location in Venice. Sean is a Venice local. His roots run deeply beneath this storied beach neighborhood of Los Angeles. Once he got wind we were scouting out locations, he genially offered to show us around his neighborhood, all from the most stylish comforts of his 1964 Galaxie. The vintage convertible, perfectly symbolic of his carefree and cool beach community, gave us a moving front-row seat to everything that unfolds in what has remained one of the most interesting and dynamic parts of Los Angeles. Sean seems most comfortable representing Venice's fading, rougher roots rather than the boutique culture dominating today.

If Sean is the quintessential Dogtown local, then his Venice home represents the archetypal architecture of the neighborhood. Sean renovated the once much-smaller home with the addition of a second floor, giving his family of two boys and a lovely wife, Stella, more room to grow. Their kitchen, living room, and dining room now coalesce into an open-floor plan crowned by a dramatic pitched ceiling, leading toward glowing views of a private front garden and backyard. Large sliding doors open onto a deck and garden of native and drought-tolerant flora. It's no surprise that the family spends as much time outside as they do inside, thanks to Venice's mild weather.

One thing you can't help but notice is a chair placed diagonally in their living room fireplace, an act that again seems to communicate Sean's "fuck it" experimental attitude. The house is otherwise a peaceful statement of domesticity, occasionally interjected by bursts of the artistic; paintings and photography juxtaposed against neutral white walls and rock-covered surfaces give their gallery a perceptible pop. Sean shares an affinity for one piece in particular, a painting by acclaimed artist Henry Taylor. "I bought this piece from the back of Henry Taylor's car trunk."

Our friendship with Sean may have begun working together for the Line Hotel, but even before then, we admired his work in interiors and landscape design. Beyond the hotel, his portfolio is well represented by residential and commercial projects for Roy Choi and many celebrity clients. He's considered a star but doesn't wear this reputation in any noticeable fashion, and he seems uninterested in any notion of celebrity. When we asked Sean to be part of this book, his first question was, "Who will be in it?" At first, we thought his question was intended to scout out whether he'd be joining other esteemed and recognizable names. But it was only when we told him the impetus for the book was to fill its pages with friends and collaborators—the community of creatives we consider symbolic of everything we believe Poketo represents—did Sean offer a simple affirmation that represents how he operates.

"I'm in."

SPARTINA
BAKERI

OAKLEAF
HYDRANGEA

ASCLEPIAS
BUTTERFLY
BUSH

BALLERINA
ROSE
BUSH

CHASING THE SUN

Along with designing environments, Sean also architects landscapes. We remember him describing to us that when you plant things, over time they move to different spots, literally. Plants and flowers grow and bloom, we get that, but we love that they are like people, moving, growing, and chasing the sun. Sean and Stella's love for plants extends into another business that they own together, Flowerboy Project: part café, retail shop, and florist. They have a couple of locations in LA offering joy and sunshine for all who enter. We asked Sean to share some of his favorite plants and flowers with us. We imagined Sean, Stella, and their boys, Louis and Hendrix, enjoying and playing in the garden together.

Illustration by Annie Seo

EVA GOICOCHEA

ENTREPRENEURS
Greenpoint, Brooklyn

IAN GOICOCHEA

WE FIRST MET THE GOICOCHEAS about four years ago at a party we hosted at our original Arts District retail location. Eva introduced herself as a marketer for the San Francisco–based online clothing retailer Everlane, but she was already on the cusp of setting out on her own. Even then, we sensed she was an entrepreneurial spirit who was only just getting started.

We got to know Eva better after inviting her over to our house to talk shop. We'd already gleaned that we shared a love for branding, marketing, and other entrepreneurial topics, but our burgeoning bond was forever established when Eva noticed our two Shih Tzu dogs. She ended up one-upping us that evening, revealing she was the parent of *three* Shih Tzus (along with two cats), a bona fide animal lover with an especially soft spot for rescuing strays. Maybe business brought us together, but it was our dogs that made us friends. During the course of the evening, we gushed over our animals, compared notes, and convinced Eva to lead what would become the first of many Poketo workshops about branding.

All good things must come to an end, and Eva and Ian would eventually leave Los Angeles to set up base in New York after helping launch Tinker, a minimalist modern watch company—Eva as the brand's marketer, Ian the engineer ensuring the fashionable was functional. Not satisfied with just one brand, Eva would eventually go on to cofound and launch Maude, a sex-positive, minimalist-styled, gender-neutral sex essentials company that has garnered a lot of press for reshaping the category as an inclusive experience.

"My mother, who raised me primarily by herself, has a deep sense of curiosity and fearlessness that has really shaped how I approach life. She has always been social, with a wide-open heart and the ability to make friends anywhere, while also being comfortable spending time alone. She reminds me to be centered, fearless, and at peace, no matter what's before me."

Over the years they've also been extremely gracious in inviting us to stay with them at their brick-lined Brooklyn apartment whenever we're in New York. Like most entrepreneurs, Eva and Ian work nonstop, attached to hectic professional schedules that could easily spill into their personal lives. Whether consciously or unconsciously, they've created the antithesis of their always-moving-forward lifestyle with an apartment that invites calm and warmth. Eva and Ian have a knack for decorating spaces with an understated modernist's eye, and their airy and monochromatic furnishings and décor do a fine job of straddling the minimalist and cozy.

An enviable amount of natural light fills the corner apartment, making the space feel much larger than its actual dimensions. A canopy of treetops outside their living room windows creates the illusion of an outdoor garden, without any of the upkeep. You'll often find the couple sitting together at their long picnic-style table throughout the day, a central spot where work and play intermingle. We've shared more than a few memorable meals together there; it's where conversation and collaboration seem to be the foregone conclusion born of the atmosphere.

A neutral palette permits small, warm details to tell the story of the couple's interests and passions: a framed Georgia O'Keeffe x Brooklyn Museum print hinting at Eva's New Mexico roots, the melted wax–covered candleholder revealing romantic evenings past, thoughtfully placed pet beds to keep their most beloved comfortable and happy, and a photo of Eva's mother from when she was younger, capturing the same warm smile her daughter inherited.

Although it's always hard to say goodbye when friends move away, we've remained connected with Eva and Ian over the years, sharing updates about our pets and advice about the business of business—the logistics of customer service, shipping, and warehousing, and the odds and ends of operating your own brand. We proudly carry Maude kits at our Poketo shops today, an endorsement of what we believe is an incredible brand and in support of a friendship that has spanned work and play throughout the years.

LUKAS PEET

INDUSTRIAL DESIGNER

Vancouver, Canada

THE WORD THAT WILL continually pop into our heads while touring ANDlight's 5,000-square-foot industrial space studio is *flexible*. These walls once housed a lumber-processing plant, followed by additional past lives as a wood workshop, a musical jam space, and an artist space. Lukas and his two founding partners, Matt Davis and Caine Heintzman, converted the once-raw space into ANDlight, a lighting company whose inventive designs always seem to exist at the inflection point where less becomes more.

"Caine and I design independently, allowing our brand a bit more of a diverse aesthetic and not just inhabiting one person's vision. Which we think is good because it also gives the brand stability; there are people who like his lights, and there are people who like my lights, creating a range of customers. That diversity really helps," Lukas says.

Loosely divided into a studio, assembly/production space, showroom, and fulfillment center, there's little separation between each operational area. It's a situation we can really relate to; Poketo would probably benefit from dividing our studio/office teams from operations. Admittedly it isn't always ideal to work in a space where the retail and design teams have to operate within the same space as fulfillment and warehousing. But we agree about the numerous benefits of the "all under one roof" approach: Teams remain tightly knit, proximity promotes interaction, and the coordination between teams remains easier to orchestrate. A cooperative flow of activity and energy connects each department. Nowhere is the ideal more visible than within ANDLight's large assembly room. Mammoth plywood tables sit surrounded by industrial shelves stocked with materials, tools, and machinery. Here team members piece together lighting fixtures with differing degrees of movement and purpose. Adjacent, a humble medley of affordable materials, notably plywood and corrugated plastic panels, comes together to demarcate another area intended for design and office operations. (We use

"I believe it's really important to find ways to continue to train our creativity throughout our lives. It's about making time, like training for a marathon."

many of the same inexpensive materials at Poketo for the similar purpose of creating privacy while inviting natural light.) A little farther toward the front-facing windows, a floor display showcases ANDLight's entire catalog of products, adjoined by a large conference table intended for client meetings and presentations.

From this communal table, Lukas will fill us in about his time studying at the Design Academy Eindhoven before cofounding ANDLight with his friends, eventually revealing yet another parallel between our two companies: the desire for control. Lukas desired to control everything he designed, including the supervision of their production, how designs would be marketed, and ultimately the ability to adapt quickly and efficiently in response to the market—ideals stemming from a childhood observing his jeweler father, who always emphasized pursuing creativity steadied by pragmatic considerations.

"Sometimes I'll see another designer's lighting fixture, and I'll appreciate it for its details and thoughtful execution. But I also have to view design from the perspective of a business owner, identifying what may or may not sell," explains Lukas. "I also believe if you're a designer, it's your job to be creative. And being creative means making new things."

While *new* is an operative word of emphasis, it's not meant to imply the pursuit of novelty. Lukas just means to emphasize the importance of an additive, forward progression to design, where an idea begins where another last left off: "I believe in never starting from zero again!"

Spending time with Lukas ignites a passionate response from us because we most identify with creatives who've forged their own path in life. When we began Poketo, we didn't immediately know how to define the ideals of "art everyday" into the context of something larger, but we knew we had to start somewhere. We'd build upon every small success and springboard from there to yet another project. So wallets became housewares, which in turn became apparel, which then turned into our branded workshops, and eventually led to partnerships with other companies and designers. In Lukas we've identified a fellow adherent to the practice of making, doing, and collaborating, someone who squeezes in efforts in ten- to fifteen-minute increments to make ideas become reality.

"I believe it's really important to find ways to continue to train our creativity throughout our lives. It's about making time, like training for a marathon. You might have a busy life, but if you want to cover the distance, you have to find those ten to fifteen minutes here and there to build creative mileage. In the end all those small efforts add up. And on numerous occasions those efforts have turned into ideas for a new light or design for ANDLight."

ADAM
J. KURTZ

ARTIST AND AUTHOR
Williamsburg, Brooklyn

ADAM AND MITCHELL'S Brooklyn dwelling is the quintessential small New York apartment, complete with exposed brick walls, manifesting the "making it work" attitude the city is renowned for. Visiting this newly married couple's flat on the south side of Williamsburg is a reminder of how the spirit of a home is determined not by square footage but by the care and consideration of its occupants. And if there's anything we found true while visiting Adam and Mitchell over the summer, it's that this New York couple loves their small space almost as much as they do one another.

It's become common knowledge that Brooklyn has changed considerably in the last several decades from its working-class roots, becoming the destination for subjectively "affordable" rentals in New York among young creatives priced out of Manhattan one bridge over. But even with the brushstrokes of gentrification painting over much of the city's industrial past, there's still a perceptible old-school feeling inhabiting these parts.

This is a holdout section of the city where one can still find older gentlemen playing dominoes outside under the shade of trees. The air here seems perpetually perfumed with music, a lingering percussion that fades in and out while we navigate the sidewalks. Neighbors still like to keep their doors open in anticipation of friends and family dropping by, with private conversations spilling out in clipped snippets into public earshot.

When we finally climb up the stairs and slide in through Adam and Mitchell's front door, the reality of a New York floor plan comes clearly into focus. Rooms here have to fill multipurpose roles. The kitchen and living room are combined into a single room, and look onto a cozy bedroom baked bright with sunlight and enlivened by colorful bedding. Adam's home office is announced by the unmistakable glow of neon promising all who enter "Gifts." The long, narrow room, which hosts all of Adam's operations as a creative and business owner, is occupied almost entirely by shelves and a long desk across its span. Adam is first and foremost a super talented graphic designer and illustrator, and the author of several published books, but we're blown away to realize he operates his highly successful online gift business— mailing out books, pins, and stickers of his own design to fans around the world—from these modest confines. Adam and Mitchell, a gifted writer, are both at the stage in life where they're still building and growing, personally and professionally. It's a loving and collaborative relationship, and they work throughout the day elbow to elbow.

It's no exaggeration to say it's Adam's curatorial eye and collector's heart on display throughout this simple and cozy apartment. *Things Are What You Make of Them* is the title of one of Adam's books, and here the idiom seems to be put into practice unpretentiously. Personal work and ephemera collected over the years color the walls with texture: a pin collection peppering two-thirds of a large bulletin board like an assemblage of emojis made real, or the precariously stacked

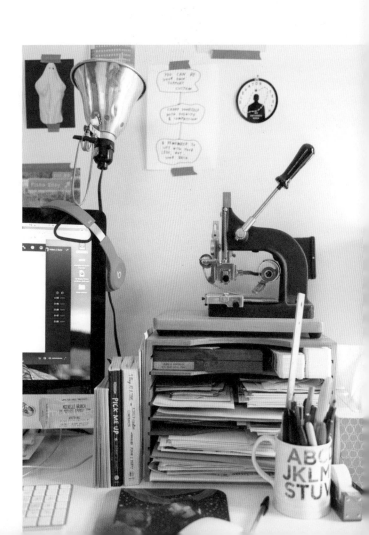

pile of his books translated into numerous languages, revealing his global audience. Photos and postcards suspended by string and clothespins over their bed serve as a timeline of the who, what, when, and where of their life together. There's a never-ending compulsion to lean in for a closer look at every detail.

We got to know Adam by the simple act of reaching out and proposing a collaboration (it's amazing how effective "Hello, let's work together" can be as a business strategy and the start of a friendship). Even before connecting, Poketo had already been carrying his books at the store for some time. His work is rather popular among our own staff, who are charmed by his signature style of confessional, hand-drawn quotes and illustrations that deliver on both the internet meme front and, more importantly, on a genuinely personal, authentic, and relatable level. Adam has a gift for illustrating and penning heartfelt messages that avoid sentimental tropes and instead inspire gratitude that someone else feels the same way, too.

How fortunate we feel we were able to eventually host a book reading with Adam at Poketo. Adam's fans came out in droves to listen to him read from his book *Things Are What You Make of Them*. Like us, everyone was charmed by his adorable vain affectation, a personality that plays up perfectly to the self-described multi-hat-wearing "designer–author–illustrator–creative director–writer–small press" brand his business is built upon. Adam is a strong personality with a tendency to "say it like it is" and is never one to mince words, but he's also shockingly kind and somebody who believes in random acts of kindness. We'll never forget the excitement we witnessed when our store manager rushed over to tell us with wide-eyed joy, "Adam J. Kurtz came into the shop today! He gave me a pin off his jacket!" He's a harbinger of happiness who has the power to change someone's day with only a small token of earnest encouragement.

ONE NICE THING ABOUT A
CREATIVE SPACE IS THAT
IT CAN BE ANYWHERE YOU
WANT, INCLUDING RIGHT HERE:

ADELE TETANGCO

FASHION ENTREPRENEUR
Vancouver, Canada

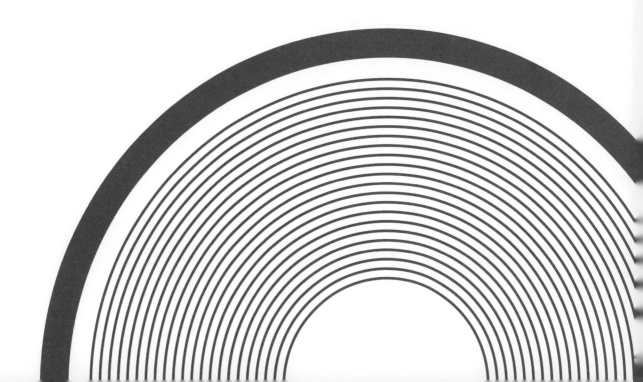

IF THERE'S ANYTHING we've learned over the years running Poketo, it's that projects and partnerships are rarely a one-and-done affair. So much of what we've accomplished and the friendships we've made over the years can be attributed to the domino effect: one thing leading to another. For example, if we had never attended an indie designer fashion tradeshow in 2017, we might have never met Adele, the cofounder of Vancouver-based online retailer and tastemaker Garmentory.

Adele lives just outside of Vancouver in a suburban townhome she shares with her husband and two daughters, eighteen-year-old Jayme and six-year-old Cielo. In contrast to their vivacious personalities, the interior of their three-story home is mostly expressed in varying shades of white; only a few instances of color burst into view by way of the family's collection of art, books, and plants. Like pages in a coloring book only just begun, strategically colored sections seem to highlight only the most meaningful of details in this home. The soft and spare minimalism of their shared spaces gives way to the personalized confines of their bedrooms, where color has more license. Cielo's bedroom reveals a coterie of soft playthings and intricate decorative touches that reveal the apples haven't fallen far from the tree.

The living room and kitchen are Adele's primary domain; it's where she operates while working from home a couple of times a week. A sensual Verner Panton chair sits at a desk reserved for her laptop, while a large canvas of the lyrics to "One Love" by Nas, painted in cursive, fills the adjacent wall. It's a deceptive decorative element laced with f-bombs that provides an amusing contrast to its restrained minimalist surroundings. Adele explains this was an intentional choice in hopes of creating a sanctuary from the everyday grind.

It's not uncommon in our world to establish a business relationship ahead of a personal one. In the case of Adele, we first established a working relationship at a Los Angeles designer and trade show she organized under the banner of Garmentory. When we opened our fourth store, we were able to return the favor and invite Adele to work with us on a showcase of brands and designers we love. We wanted Garmentory to be our first showcase. We ended up cocurating somewhere in the neighborhood of forty independent fashion designers. But in hindsight, it was Adele's picks that stood out as the most memorable for the inaugural event.

Looking back, Adele came into our lives perhaps when we most needed someone like her. At the time, Poketo was weathering a particularly challenging period of uncertainty. As our original shop in the Los Angeles Arts District faced imminent closure, we were concurrently working on the opening of a replacement in the ROW DTLA. Nothing seemed definitive and assurances were few. The stress could have sunk us, but meeting Adele gave us an unexpected shot of buoyancy.

The Poketo Project Space was still only a conceptual hope rather than physical reality when we began plotting our cosponsored event with Adele and Garmentory. Our new store wasn't complete yet, and we were still tangled in the morass of red tape required to procure a city permit to host our opening event. To makes things worse, we were also juggling a team of contractors responsible for turning the raw unfinished space into our new store. As the worst of our doubts began creeping in, Adele would always seem to call just at the right time, listening to our worries, and eventually rallying our spirits with a "we can do it!" pep talk. Adele is someone whose optimism cannot and will not be denied.

In the end, the grand opening of Poketo Project Space and the Garmentory pop-up was a success, thanks in great part to Adele. She and her small but motivated team rallied to contact every vendor and organize everything required for the pop-up to happen on time. Adele went as far as to come in to help us merchandise the shop, an act far beyond any expectations and requirements, but reflective of her all-hands-on-deck personality.

Adele comes back to Los Angeles regularly enough that we can plan to see one another throughout the year. We're bound by the memories of working on the launch together, but also by the commonality of navigating the responsibilities of operating a retail business and all the pressures that come with it. What's developed isn't just a business relationship, but one of mutual respect and understanding—a friendship among peers born of sweat, laughter, and tears (and maybe the occasional dirty rap lyrics).

I TAKE *MIRROR SELFIES* BECAUSE I LOVE THE ENVIRONMENTS THAT I'M IN... IT'S MORE ABOUT THE SPACE THAN THE LOOK. ALTHOUGH, I LOVE THE LOOK.

YOU ARE A VISION

Adele's personal Instagram account is an unpolished, day-in-the-life look at an entrepreneur meeting designers and trying on new collections. She often snaps selfies with the clothes she's in love with and the spaces she's in. It's a recurring theme from her account, and we love that she brings her own personality to fashion. Here are some of her favorite looks, clothing, and spaces in the selfies she has taken over the years.

Illustration by Annie Seo

TERRI
CHIAO

ARTISTS
Bushwick, Brooklyn

ADAM
FREZZA

ARTIST COUPLE TERRI AND ADAM live together, work together, and raise a daughter together—lives so intertwined, their names have merged into the singular portmanteau Chiaozza (*CHOW-zah*, pronounced with the verve of "yowza!"). Every facet of their lives embodies the whimsical, playful, spontaneous, and explorative, and walking into their wondrous Bushwick loft corroborates the sense that these two intensely imaginative people have found in each other their favorite and forever playmate.

If you were at Coachella 2017, you might have partied in the enormous bio-organic sculpture garden they designed, a fluorescent forest of bulbous forms reminiscent of succulent plants exploded to momentous scale. Our first exposure to Chiaozza's work was of a more modest size, though no less wondrous. We spotted *Suspended Confetti*, individually decorated ceramic fragments hovering between two round mirrors, at Sight Unseen's Offsite 2016 in New York, and were instantly wowed. The lengths seemed to resemble the limp luminescent arms of a giant jellyfish, but one inspired by the '80s palette of an Ettore Sottsass hallucination. We walked around it and peered underneath, all the while feeling the urge to completely immerse ourselves inside its otherworldly kinetic energy of color and form. Now, years later, this book would provide the opportunity for us to share this memory of awe and wonder in person with the artists themselves.

Some artists create a delineation between work and life, but Terri and Adam's world is an unapologetically bold and bright amalgamation swirled together. Each brings a distinct set of talents to the table—Terri, the trained architect turned conceptual artist guided by a measured design methodology; Adam, the self-described "frustrated carpenter" and sculptor. Terri notes they bonded over the recognition they'd both operated along the outskirts of their respective subjects of study, attributing the success of their partnership to their outsider perspective. "He's a builder and painter, and I'm a drawer and architect," Terri says. They've used these differences to their advantage, while also converging on a shared love of nature as inspiration.

Terri and Adam's approach to making art together as Chiaozza is a dynamic of push and pull, compromise and collaboration, and always perceived as an additive rather than subtractive process. Adam equates it to dancing with a partner, each step back and forth eventually synchronizing their moves as one. What's enviable is how this couple has adopted playful strategies to solve serious problems. "We do lots of different drawing games where we build off of each other's shapes, recognizing what comes out of the exchange is not like anything either of us would have created independently."

The vitality of their partnership explodes into focus within their 750-square-foot loft, the most personal manifestation of what Terri describes as the heart of their work: "creating an experience." And what an experience it is!

Inside the walls of their brick-lined space, their philosophical commitment to play as paramount to their process is undeniably visible. Inhabited by two full-size plywood structures—one a stand-alone cabin, the other a lofted treehouse bedroom—Terri and Adam's compulsion to build the life they've imagined is on full display. "I feel like it opens up your mind to not be so dependent on consumer culture . . . like buying furniture and then getting rid of it. I think when you can imagine what you would want and build it yourself, you become more thoughtful about choosing things, and those things in your home become much more valuable," Terri says as she surveys their handmade furniture. Guided by their DIY manifesto, they've transformed the blank canvas of a wide-open industrial space into their own miniature village of sorts. The impression is of a giant diorama, an interior playground where the couple play with their infant daughter, Tove, and their cat, Giro, surrounded by a medley of weird and wonderful objects they've collected or made themselves over the years.

Adam admits the collaborative realities of cohabitation required a little experimentation at first: "It was originally a little more minimal when I first moved in. I'd bring weird objects from my apartment into her place, but we were eventually able to weave together our styles after I realized not all of my tchotchkes needed to come over right away." But don't worry, Adam's assembly of weird sculptures and other artistic endeavors eventually found a refuge in a separate studio located only a block away. The extra studio has given the pair a space to work on demanding and rewarding projects for the likes of Nike and Uniqlo, bringing in enough income that they no longer need to rent out the "Cabin in a Loft," their small house-inside-a-house structure. Future plans include purchasing land outside the city to give their daughter a place to explore nature, and to build structures intended to facilitate additional art and design projects, including something they're already calling the Parallel House—two structures aligned in parallel for live and work environments in the countryside.

So often you hear the ideal of "people making a life together," but Terri and Adam have literally constructed a uniquely creative career and lifestyle predicated on their partnership and mutual support. When we started Poketo, we began with the idea that art and design have the power to deliver daily moments of happiness to others. Chiaozza operate with this ideal in everything they do: "There's so many things you could choose to put into the world, so why not try to put the positive things?"

CHIAOZZA

A PARALLEL LIFE

Something we love about Terri and Adam is that they collaborate on everything they do. With their artwork, they often do an exquisite corpse, handing artwork back and forth, each adding their own contribution to what ends up being a unified piece. One of their dreams is to build the Parallel House, a house and studio paralleling each other—a place that is seamless for their art and life where they can give Tove a wonderful home. When we met, they were talking about this magical home and studio being in Upstate New York. In this collage they did together, you can see their vision with one change. Instead of the mountains and rivers of Upstate, they envisioned the Parallel House on the ocean.

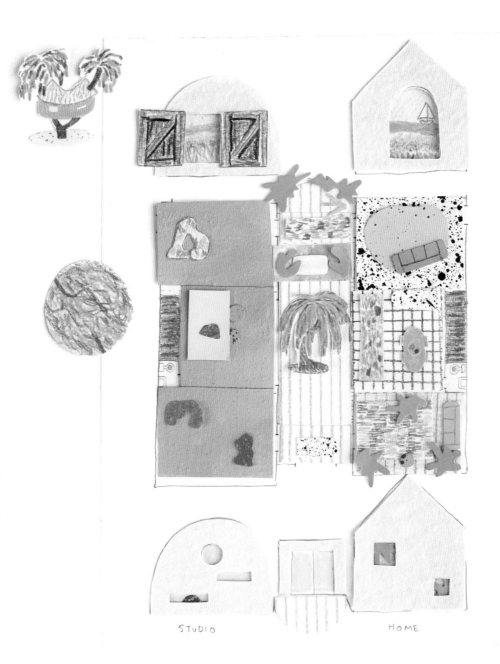

STUDIO   HOME

JEAN
LEE

DESIGNERS
Red Hook, Brooklyn

DYLAN
DAVIS

VISITING OUR FRIENDS and longtime collaborators Jean and Dylan always offers the promise of a small but dependably memorable adventure. Where normally a taxi or subway ride might suffice for visiting other friends in New York, the quickest and most fun route out to Jean and Dylan's Brooklyn studio is made by boat—specifically the IKEA Brooklyn ferry departing from Wall Street's Pier 11 in Manhattan. We always look forward to the scenic half-hour ride across the choppy waters, delivering Instagram-worthy views of both Manhattan and Brooklyn from either side. The buildup of anticipation as we near the harbor and our friends' studio is genuine—a reminder of how the journey adds to an appreciation of the eventual destination.

Thankfully, once on shore it's only a short walk from the pier along the waterfront to Jean and Dylan's design studio. Operating under the nom de guerre Ladies & Gentlemen, the couple's business is housed within a formidable brick building with a multitude of soot-black shutters, arched windows, and doorways, duplicated with the repetitive composition of a simple song. It's hard to imagine the bustling creative space was once occupied by the back-breaking labor of Brooklyn's waterfront industries, but if you close your eyes, the seashore's past can creep back into the imagination. Jean informs us Red Hook remains one of the last neighbor-hoods where artists and designers can still carve out an affordable space to create and collaborate. Once-abandoned industrial buildings are now sub-divided into a multitude of raw spaces, including our friends' 2,000-square-foot studio. It's not formally a live/work studio, but plenty of life and work unfolds within its walls. The studio interior is decorated with a harmonious collection of random samples, scraps, found objects, design explorations, and bespoke furnishings the couple has collected. The organization allows them to literally "grab things from the shelf" to piece together prototypes informed by the tactile rather than by concepts alone. "We've collected a variety of art glass samples over the years, but for the longest time we never knew what to do with them. Then two years later they became the foundation of an idea for a light fixture. The material became something like a language for us to use. We keep stuff around to continue to speak to us," Dylan explains.

L&G's work today falls somewhere between lighting and kinetic sculpture, abstract geometric mobiles representing functional studies in color, balance, movement, and even sound. The multitude and diversity of their work seems to represent the efforts of a collective rather than a mere couple: mismatched and colorful chandeliers hanging with the mysterious purpose of a Rube Goldberg contraption, wind chimes assembled with the free-flowing composition of a '60s jazz ensemble improvisation, a luminous and layered sconce inspired by the late-1800s Russian artist Kazimir Malevich. The mobiles they designed for Poketo use a medley of metal, glass, brass, and wood, conjuring a heightened attention to simplicity comparable to a traditional Japanese aesthetic.

Their style has evolved over the years, but Jean notes the constant in their work is an observable commitment to offering an experiential relationship between object and person.

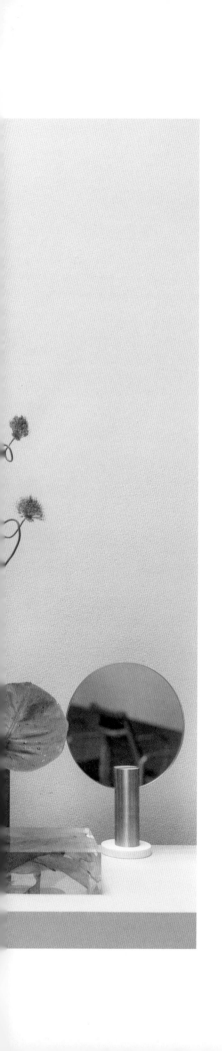

LINDSEY HAMPTON

CERAMICIST AND GRAPHIC DESIGNER
Vancouver, Canada

IT WAS LOVE AT FIRST SIGHT when Lindsey's ceramics first appeared on our Instagram feed years ago, each subsequent swipe revealing architectural vessels embellished with the pastel blush of an imaginary new wave sunset—some freckled with texture, others accessorized with whimsical touches of waves, wiggles, and rings. A kindred spirit, albeit one operating from hundreds of miles away, Lindsey eventually became one of our favorite collaborators, responsible for designing several Poketo Exclusive planters, mugs, and vessels, which we sell at our stores today.

If you ask us what makes Lindsey's work so special, we'd cite the polyamorous relationship she has with creativity as a whole; her ability to connect the dots between disciplines colors everything she does. Whether it's working as a graphic designer, ceramics artist, musician, or photographer, Lindsey imbues each medium with a remarkable gift for balancing proportion, negative space, and color. It's no surprise her work is rooted in graphic design, skills established well before clay entered her life. Look carefully and it's easy to note the confident precision of someone who knows her way around Photoshop, with many of her ceramic pieces embellished with exact applications of color and pattern that heighten but never overpower their form. Lindsey's talent is the ability to wield spontaneity and control with equal adeptness, regardless of which facet of her creativity she is exploring. As individuals prone to boredom if restrained by repetition, we admire when creatives like Lindsey keep their work and lives from falling into a formulaic tempo—it's no wonder our collaborations have felt so natural.

"Making ceramics is physically the opposite of designing on the computer, but it still requires using the same part of my brain. I like the challenge of designing in three dimensions. It feels comfortable because it still utilizes all the skills I use in graphic design—'Oh, I'm doing exactly the same thing but that end result was completely different'—so I didn't find the transition to clay overwhelming."

Lindsey credits her upbringing in a small, rural area on Vancouver Island surrounded by forest, acquainted with darkness, appreciative of nature and water, as greatly influential; childhood memories of seemingly limitless hours left alone with the freedom to explore, face fears, and topple boredom color her creative perspective today. These days she's found a balance professionally and geographically, living in a city where she can disappear into a forest within a half-hour bicycle ride and then reappear to enjoy the cultural offerings of a large city. "I love being here in Vancouver. I know you can't be in two places at once, but I guess if I get super rich, I could have two homes." It's easy to see how this desire to be "here" and also "there" manifests in the duality of her careers. "I have to set goals for myself as a designer and ceramicist. I'll tell myself to focus on design work until this time, and only then will I allow myself to go to the studio, leaving my design mindset at home."

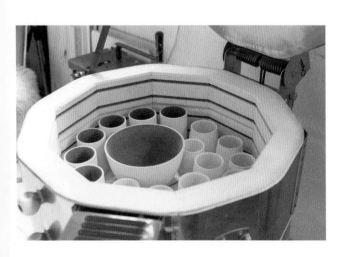

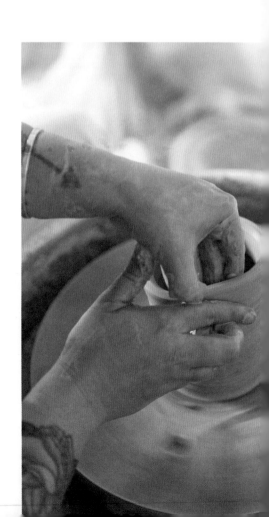

Lindsey's studio is located in the heart of Vancouver, perpendicular to one of the city's more bustling commercial avenues. She says the ten-minute commute by foot or bike from home to her studio, along a tree-shaded string of boutique eateries and shops, is a perpetual source of inspiration as she transitions from a graphic designer to an artist working with clay.

Stepping into Lindsey's studio, we're immediately taken aback by the unusually tidy and organized workspace dedicated to such a messy medium. It's a small space, about 500 square feet, but it is part of a greater communal building for artists. Everything is wide open to view and arranged with a systematic attention to the process in which she operates. Most ceramicists we know work within the confines of what we call functional chaos. Not Lindsey—her space reveals she hasn't completely left her design mind at home. "I do clean up a lot and run a pretty clean studio. But it's still messy and I would like to try one day to have everything in one spot," she admits. The space brings to mind what a Memphis Group–style studio might look like today, decorated with bright pops of color, geometric shapes, and precise lines and grids.

Lindsey's work may hint of molds, but everything she makes is formed by hand, with the only assistance provided by her potter's wheel. From a quiet corner, she spins clay into various architectural vessels, surrounded by tools neatly organized across a pegboard to her right and a shelf of pieces awaiting the next step to the left. She eventually applies graphics and gradients to each piece with the deft accuracy of a machine. This is not to say her work looks manufactured—far from it; the organic characteristics of clay are always noticeable in her pieces. But the graphics and colors she uses are unbelievable in detail, and reveal subtle nuances of shade and intensity.

A lone pink table crowned with an overhead green lamp holds court in the middle of the small room; it's here Lindsey takes meetings or reads, enjoys a meal, or occasionally catches up on emails. If the table is the brain of the room, the large kiln sitting to the right is the room's heart burning bright. "I think of the kiln as similar to a printing press: You do something, you send it off somewhere, and you get the results. There's something about not completely knowing until the very end that's magical. Any ceramicist will tell you opening the kiln is always the most exciting part of the process. Even if it's full of the exact same mug that you've just made over and over and over again, there's still an element of chance."

JUST WARMING UP

Creativity comes in all forms. When we asked Lindsey how she gets started on projects, she said she often just plays around with materials, composition, and colors to get creative juices flowing. Sometimes it's painting, drawing, or sitting down with a ball of clay. She's a big believer in a "just make and see where it goes" philosophy. She made these icons to warm up and quickly test out ideas to see if they are worth spending time on for finished pieces. Whether for graphic design work or making ceramics, these exercises tap into the same part of her creativity, and ultimately end up as thoughtful, cohesive projects.

STEPHANIE FORSYTHE

ARCHITECTS
Vancouver, Canada

TODD
MACALLEN

STEPHANIE AND TODD are standing high above us on an electric scissor lift, stretching a final expanse of honeycomb paper to complete an enormous partition across a corner of their vast East Vancouver studio. They're showing us how rapidly their origami-inspired softwall and softseating systems can be adapted into a myriad of shapes to create environments of both intimate and colossal scale. The sinuous bark-hued softwall they're currently arranging is enormous, stacked three walls high, soaring nearly to the top of the 20-foot ceiling. It's easy to imagine ourselves standing in the desert slot canyons of the Zion Narrows in Utah or among towering old-growth Sitka spruce in the Pacific Rim National Park Reserve. The arrangement takes on the monumental footprint of a Richard Serra installation, but rendered in the soft undulation of paper rather than unforgiving steel. These flexible environmental designs were our first introduction to the architectural and nature-inspired work of molo (Stephanie and Todd's company) years ago, but seeing them in person is rather awesome.

We have to admit it wasn't until this book that Stephanie and Todd would cross the threshold from distant acquaintances to friends. As noted, we already admired their work, but we didn't really know the people responsible for it. But even though our relationship was only at a nascent state, the couple was enthusiastically responsive about inviting us up to their cavernous 20,000-square-foot studio. The pair gutted and converted the two-story former industrial structure into a true live/work environment with

"We tend to meander back and forth, doing things incrementally, then arriving at a point together."

its own residential wing. The light-filled, white-washed first floor operates as a perfect blank canvas to show-case the studio's multitude of designs, a sparse aesthetic dedicated to inanimate objects, with the second floor furnished to serve its occupants.

Throughout the day with Stephanie and Todd, we'd also become privy to the workings of a couple operating in synchrony and in recognition of their different strengths. Maybe in this way the two-story architecture of their home/office mirrors the two stories of personalities within: Todd the analytic and organized mind focused on the specifics upstairs, Stephanie dedicated to the big picture and representing the front-facing impression on behalf of their studio downstairs. It's remarkably very sim-ilar to the partnership we've established operating Poketo as a couple with complementary personalities and skills.

"It ends up being good because we have different per-spectives and different strengths. We end up covering a lot more ground than we would by ourselves. My flaws can become an asset," says Stephanie.

"When we work together, we can see the things at a deeper level . . . from a perspective coming from in between who we both are," Todd chimes in. "And it's not just working in separate paths and then coming together. I don't think it's interesting to have discussion without feedback, or to have discussion with only pedestrian agreement to be polite."

One of the greatest rewards of working on this book, beyond visiting the private realms and working spaces of people we admire, was seeing people motivated by the same ideals echo many of the same challenges and con-cerns we've experienced operating Poketo. "We never aspired to become anyone's boss. I really didn't want a client; I didn't want to become a landlord. But I want to make things." Stephanie's confession represents the conundrum of professional creatives operating their own businesses: We don't want to manage people, and we'd rather be left alone to just create. But operating a busi-ness requires adaption and flexibility, no different from the elastic design of molo's expandable paper partitions.

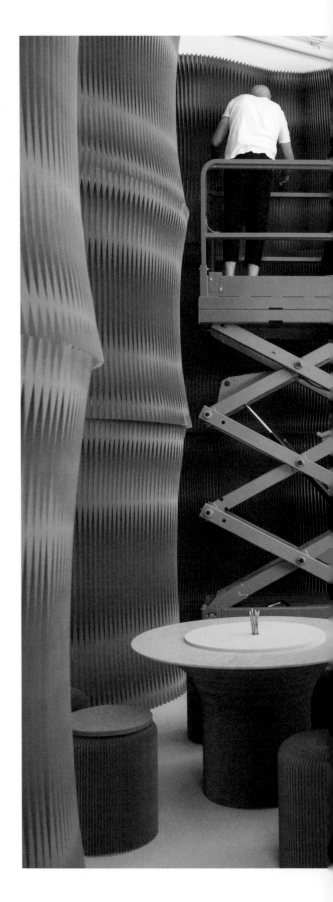

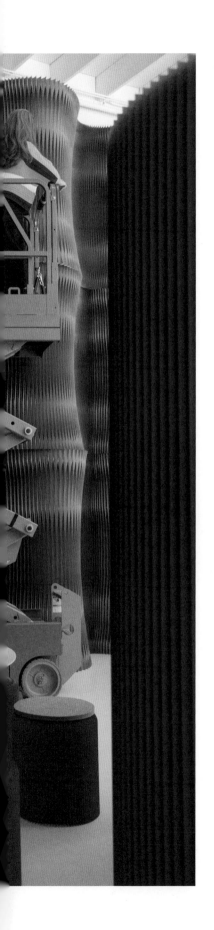

TINA ROTH EISENBERG

ENTREPRENEUR
Boerum Hill, Brooklyn

HANGING OUT WITH A FRIEND at a party, a restaurant, a bar, or their home invites certain facets of our personalities to come to light. Observing someone at work, or working with them, can reveal a different side altogether. Our friend Tina Eisenberg's invitation to visit her Brooklyn studio allowed us to witness the microcosm from which she orchestrates not just one but several creative endeavors. We already knew Tina as a friend and collaborator, a human being gifted with a warm smile and a consummate eye for smart design. Now we got to see Tina, the successful entrepreneur behind CreativeMornings, Tattly, and a coworking project called Friends Work Here, operating within her element.

Tina has been a staple of the creative scene in DUMBO, Brooklyn, since long before the neighborhood earned its trendy acronym standing for Down Under the Manhattan Bridge Overpass. She's since moved on to establish a two-story presence within the Invisible Dog, an artists' building located in the nearby neighborhood of Boerum Hill, an area teeming with the activity of a multitude of creative companies. From these two floors Tina confidently leads CreativeMornings—a mammoth global enterprise supporting and spotlighting artists, designers, makers, entrepreneurs, and thought leaders through a monthly series of morning talks. Creative-Mornings began with just Tina. She'd personally invite speakers from a myriad of industries to lead free, intimate talks in New York City revolving around their motivations, challenges, and creative epiphanies. Creative-Mornings has since expanded into a 1,500-volunteer operation across 200 cities (and counting) in more than 65 countries.

But it was Tattly—the temporary tattoo design company Tina founded in 2011—that most parallels our own beginnings as an artist-oriented wallet brand and brought us together as collaborators. Tina originally founded Tattly to offer her young daughter a tasteful alternative to the garish temporary tattoos marketed to kids. The fun designs exploded in popularity and are now sold around the globe—including at Poketo shops—an example of how a small idea can be nurtured into something substantial with lots of effort, a little bit of luck, and the binding force of connections between kindred spirits.

Both of Tina's studios are arranged as open floor plans, each buzzing and bustling with teams working from computers and collaborating across communal spaces. She's arranged her offices in uniform rows of white desks sitting across the warm and worn wooden floors of the old building. The brick walls are washed white to match the vast expanse of dry-erase board covered with strategies and plans organized by quarterly goals. It's a highly organized space, with shelves packed neatly with inventory, yet one infused with playfulness and collaboration, all characterizing what it's like to work for and with Tina. We loved spotting a door decorated with various

shout-outs to employees and collaborators, and celebrating a variety of events, like dog adoptions or joyous announcements. Bright orange seating dots the office. A sizable corner is dedicated to relaxed and comfortable powwows (complete with a "Hey" sign overhead). How can we ignore the swing attached to the ceiling intended for impromptu swing-and-daydream sessions? The signs here all point toward a company where fun is a by-product of everyone's efforts. As fellow passionate proponents of the "work hard, play hard" ethos, it's no wonder working with Tina has always felt natural and easy. Birds of a feather, flocking together.

If Tina's offices in Brooklyn represent the enthusiastic efforts of a collaborative community, her home nearby seems dedicated to a quieter aspect of her life, which she shares with her two children. It's a calm refuge of books, art, and design objects complemented with the occasional lovingly drawn messages to "Mommy." She reminisces about her childhood growing up in a small town in Switzerland ("a place welcoming of natural and holistic healers"), which helped shape the optimism strengthening all of her personal and professional efforts today. "As I'm getting older, I'm starting to realize how important it is to manifest what you actually really want. Unless you say what you want, the universe can't help you."

Touring her studio and observing her businesses, it's clear the core of Tina's success wells from connecting with her own feelings. "I never dread going to work because I feel it's there I can self-fulfill and put my entire self into what I'm doing. I see myself in the things I put out in the world. Who gets to do that?" It's certainly an amazing realization, one that underlines our common bond of being able to operate at the intersection of creativity and community.

TRACY WILKINSON

DESIGNER AND CERAMICIST
Mt. Washington, Los Angeles

TRACY'S MASON-BUILT 1946 brick residence is a bit of a rarity here in earthquake-prone Los Angeles, an unusual proposition of strength and vulnerability built over the span of decades by the original owner. We can actually see her home from a distance, our windows almost perfectly aligned. At sunset, the warm glow from her kitchen illuminates the silhouette of a big plant hanging from her entryway; it operates as a beacon to signal the day has ended and night has begun. I often joke we need to practice Morse code, using our lights to communicate across the canyon. But as much as we admire Tracy's home from a distance, it's up close where it becomes magical, a combination of brickwork, wood, stone, fur, and cowhide melded into a cohesive and experimental statement of an artisan's life.

We ascend the stairs to the front door, and Tracy's enormous four-legged friend, sentry, and resident napper, Brownie, greets everyone with a few leisurely wags of his tail as an admission of entry. Sunlight arrives warmly through an eastward-facing kitchen in the morning and again through the backyard near dusk, illuminating the home's flaxen-haired owner and her collection of vintage and contemporary furnishings throughout the day with an idyllic Californian radiance—the embodiment of a Fleetwood Mac song come to life.

"You try and test things, but you realize half of them don't work out . . . I am interested in the sculptural elements and discovering shape over everything else," says Tracy. It's an experimental philosophy Tracy uses to coax clay into the inimitable style of her ceramics, applied similarly to the shape of her home.

Tracy's story might have formally begun in her hometown of Yorkshire, England, followed by an education at the Royal College of Art, but it was only after immigrating to New York to pursue a career in the fashion

industry that the loose ends of her numerous talents began to weave into the pattern of a polyglot career. She'd eventually move to Los Angeles a few years later, discovering the '40s-built residence sitting in the gentle elbow of Mt. Washington—a free-spirited Los Angeles hillside community retaining a surprisingly rural vibe. Only a few minutes away from Downtown, Mt. Washington can confound first-time visitors with its untied shoelaces of paved and unpaved roads, a sparse forest of black walnut trees, and a population of coy coyotes often sighted roving between homes with architectural pedigrees attached to the likes of Richard Neutra, Gregory Ain, and John Lautner. It's a little bit country, a little bit rock 'n' roll, with some cumbia thrown in for good measure—a perfectly fine corner of Los Angeles for a Yorkshire designer drawn to the prospects of shaping a life less ordinary.

"I've always wanted a life where I can do anything, design anything, make anything that I feel like making. Opportunities and challenges make me happy and allow me to keep growing."

It was after working twenty-five years in the fashion industry and devoting nearly a decade to operating her own imprint that the English native decided to start fresh, a change that would give her the freedom to explore opportunities previously cordoned off by a full-time job. Afforded with extra time while working from home, and motivated to fashion everything to her own exacting standards, Tracy began teaching herself how to make furniture, ceramics, and homewares through the onerous process of trial and error.

From these efforts, Tracy eventually developed what would become her signature primitive pots, roughly formed fired clay embellished with crowns of waxed linen thread, an evocation of the made and unmade, injured and repaired. Within her home, a similar material dynamic exists: Panels of wood over her bed are often mistaken for the fading brushstrokes of calligraphy, when in fact the markings are the remnants of glue once used to affix a phalanx of long mirrors. "The bedroom wall was covered in skinny mirrors. I quite liked them, but I had the idea that a plain white wall in the bedroom would be better, so I began to take them off . . . I decided to abandon the idea of the white wall and keep the ply because it reminded me of a Japanese painting."

In contrast to the serene statement of her home, Tracy's garage-turned-studio floating above the foot of her driveway houses the perpetual chaos of creation, a miniature skyline of shapes and textures in varying states of completion occupying nearly every surface. Surrounded by so much texture, there's a genuine temptation to touch everything. Here, the same light entering the house is filtered through panels of translucent corrugated plastic, giving the space the neutral luminescence ideal for Tracy's work.

Looking back, we realize Tracy was the first person we thought of when we began listing people we wanted to include in this book. The ceramics she creates remain unlike any we've ever seen, and now we know the same methodical ease with which she weaves straw into clay is also represented throughout her picturesque home—a cool, natural, and easygoing vibe that is every part and parcel Tracy Wilkinson.

"You try and test things, but you realize half of them don't work out . . . I am interested in the sculptural elements and discovering shape over everything else."

ACKNOWLEDGMENTS

This book has been a dream of ours for years. It has taken this long to build the team, the community, and the friendships to make it happen. It's an honor to produce a book that features the work and lives of people we admire so dearly. Poketo has always been a catalyst for new relationships and incredible projects, and this book is no exception. There are so many people to thank and acknowledge.

To our friends featured in this book: Thank you for your excitement and enthusiasm that you brought to this project. Some of you are old friends and some are new. We feel honored to have spent time with you, that you allowed us into your homes and studios, and that you shared with us what makes a creative life worth living. We've learned so much by hearing your stories and are so happy to know this book can be an inspiration to others reading it.

Ye Rin Mok, for your incredible eye and easygoing vibe. You have a cool way of putting everyone at ease, directing the shots, and finding those magic moments. We had an amazing time collaborating with you—all the flights taken, meals shared, and moments captured together. This book is a snapshot in time that we will never forget.

Gregory Han, thank you for being the sounding board for all of our crazy ideas, for keeping us calm in the storm, and for helping us craft a personal, thoughtful narrative throughout the book. Your feedback, guidance, eloquence, and, most of all, your friendship made this project something we will cherish.

Ly Tran, for making this book come to life. We always had a vision of it in our mind, but it was your graphic design, artistry, and visual storytelling that made what was at first unimaginable, imaginable. Thanks to Vanessa Dina, whose incredible experience in book design gave everything a final polish.

Special gratitude to our editor at Chronicle Books, Camaren Subhiyah. You trusted us, you gave us the freedom to do our best work, you guided us when we were lost, your encouragement lifted us, and you were a true advocate for our vision, story, and community. Without you, this dream would not be a reality.

Maria Alcaide, for bringing this project, Poketo, and Chronicle together. You've been a fan of and advocate for Poketo for years. This project would not have seen the light of day without your grace and expertise.

Our dedicated, passionate, and hardworking team at Poketo. Thank you for making Poketo run like a well-oiled machine. Special thanks to Adrienne Fong, Cate Campbell, Eric Wang, Ly Tran, Sonya Gallardo, and Victor Gonzalez for the countless brainstorm sessions and your honest feedback. Your hard work, support, and encouragement have shaped this book.

We thank our family, friends, and all the collaborators of Poketo since our beginnings. We wish this book could have featured our entire community. We see *Creative Spaces* as a snapshot in time and a celebration of our friends, colleagues, and community. This is our first book and, hopefully, it won't be our last.

RESOURCE GUIDE

There are many designers represented in our own home and in the spaces of each person we profiled. You may have seen a sofa, table, or chair and were curious about who made it. This page is not only a resource to the individuals featured in this book but also independent creatives who are friends of Poketo and those we came across while visiting the homes and studios of *Creative Spaces*.

Ted Vadakan and Angie Myung
poketo.com

Sonoko Sakai
sonokosakai.com

Lily and Hopie Stockman
blockshoptextiles.com
lilystockman.com

David Irvin
folklor.la

Stephen Kenn and Beks Opperman
stephenkenn.com

Helen Levi
helenlevi.com

Adi Goodrich and Sean Pecknold
sing-sing.co

Brendan Ravenhill
brendanravenhill.com

Chris Manak
stonesthrow.com

Takashi Yanai
eyrc.com

Tammer Hijazi and Caitlin Mociun
bower-studios.com
mociun.com

Windy Chien
windychien.com

Shev Rush and Kevin Lane
placewares.com

Sean Knibb
knibbdesign.com
flowerboyproject.com

Eva and Ian Goicochea
getmaude.com
tinkerwatches.com

Lukas Peet
lukaspeet.com
andlight.ca

Adam J. Kurtz
adamjkurtz.com
mitchellkuga.com

Adele Tetangco
garmentory.com

Terri Chiao and Adam Frezza
eternitystew.com

Jean Lee and Dylan Davis
ladiesandgentlemenstudio.com

Lindsey Hampton
lindseyhampton.com

Stephanie Forsythe and Todd MacAllen
molodesign.com

Tina Roth Eisenberg
swiss-miss.com
creativemornings.com
tattly.com

Tracy Wilkinson
twworkshop.com

More Friends of Poketo
Eric Trine, amigomodern.com
Mimi Jung and Brian Hurewitz, earlyworkstudio.com
Shin Okuda, lookatwakawaka.com
Matthew Philip Williams, matthewmatthewmatthew.com
Tanya Aguiñiga, tanyaaguiniga.com